The
Reference Shelf®

College Sports

The Reference Shelf
Volume 93 • Number 4
H.W. Wilson
A Division of EBSCO Information Services, Inc.

Published by
GREY HOUSE PUBLISHING
Amenia, New York
2021

The Reference Shelf

Photo: iStock

The books in this series contain reprints of articles, excerpts from books, addresses on current issues, and studies of social trends in the United States and other countries. There are six separately bound numbers in each volume, all of which are usually published in the same calendar year. Numbers one through five are each devoted to a single subject, providing background information and discussion from various points of view and concluding with an index and comprehensive bibliography that lists books, pamphlets, and articles on the subject. The final number of each volume is a collection of recent speeches. Books in the series may be purchased individually or on subscription.

Publisher's Cataloging-In-Publication Data
(Prepared by The Donohue Group, Inc.)

Names: Grey House Publishing, Inc., compiler.
Title: College sports / [compiled by Grey House Publishing].
Other Titles: Reference shelf ; v. 93, no. 4.
Description: Amenia, New York : Grey House Publishing, 2021. | Includes bibliographical references and index.
Identifiers: ISBN 9781642657920 (v. 93, no. 4) | ISBN 9781642657883 (volume set)
Subjects: LCSH: College sports--United States--21st century--Sources. | College sports--Corrupt practices--United States--21st century--Sources. | College athletes--United States--21st century--Sources.
Classification: LCC GV351 .C65 2021 | DDC 796.0430973--dc23

Printed in Canada

Contents

3

Lives on the Line

4

Access to Athletics

5

Professionals and Amateurs

Student Athletes and the College Sports Debate

A 2020 study from the National Collegiate Athletic Association (NCAA), in association with the Gallup Organization, looked at the subjective outcomes for college athletes versus those who had not participated in college sports. The study looked at five measures of well-being:

Purpose—enjoying one's daily life and/or work and motivation to achieve life goals.

Social—forming healthy, supportive relationships.

Financial—effective financial management and achieving financial security.

Community—engaging with some form of community, be it a neighborhood or a community of likeminded people sharing an interest.

Physical—maintaining health and energy and effectively managing energy towards goals.

While this effort to estimate something as nebulous as well-being is necessarily subjective, the researchers felt they were able to classify respondents as "thriving," "struggling," and "suffering." Researchers have found that those who are "thriving" in multiple categories of well-being tend to have better outcomes. Individuals who are thriving in all five categories were found to be more resilient and likely to succeed in life. Overall, the study found that 12 percent of athletes were thriving in all five categories, as compared to 9 percent of nonathletes. Being a college athlete might give students a three percent better chance of achieving a healthy, satisfying, and ultimately successful life.[1]

Why do athletes thrive just a little bit more than nonathletes? The reasons are complex and involve aspects of upbringing, childhood experience, and access to resources, among other things. But proponents of collegiate and youth sports—and sport in general—might hold that participating in sports is educational in its own right. Those who take part in sport learn lessons about health and fitness, communication and teamwork, managing pressure, making relationships, taking instruction, and strategizing and planning. In other words, through sports young people learn lessons that translate into more successful efforts in other areas of their lives.

The Gallup-NCAA study is not the only research indicating lasting benefits for collegiate athletes, and there is a wealth of anecdotal evidence and testimonials that likewise speak to the benefits of sport for young people. For many years, playing sports at the high school and collegiate levels has opened up opportunities for hardworking young men and women for whom opportunities might otherwise be difficult to obtain. For some, sports can be a way out of a difficult home life. For others it can be an alternative to more dangerous or destructive paths. For many, sports represent a ticket to higher education, travel, and experiencing new things. College sports can expand minds and can enrich lives.[2]

Despite these acknowledged advantages, many players, parents, and social welfare experts have identified some serious issues with the collegiate athletics system. The primary reason is that college athletics have increasingly become a matter of money, and potential profits often result in risking the health and welfare of the college athletes.

Risks and Rewards

Student athletes are expected to be both students and athletes, but this is a difficult line to walk. Many studies and anecdotal evidence demonstrate how difficult it is to succeed equally in academics and athletics. At the highest level, playing a sport is very much like a full-time job, and students who take on this challenge, in addition to other commitments they may have in their lives, face considerable pressure and stress. The strain can be extreme and, in some cases, athletes struggle to concentrate on the educational half of their lives. Only a small percentage of collegiate athletes will go on to play professional sports or to have a related occupation. In fact, while playing a sport can impart qualities that can help a person thrive in many facets of life, studies indicate that athletes and nonathletes have similar financial outcomes.

Not all college sports are stressful or intensive. The pressure experienced by a student on a fencing team is not the same as that faced by an athlete participating in the annual March Madness competition, or playing on a top NCAA football team. The United States is unique in having an amateur sports system that attracts national and sometimes even international attention. No other country has elevated amateur athletics to this level, and this means that America's college athletes are in an unusual and unprecedented position within their society. Soon after the first intercollegiate games were organized, it became clear to educational institutions that sports wasn't just an educational benefit or a way to engage local communities but a potential gold mine. Since then, the evolution of college sports has followed the desire to maximize the revenues that this industry produces.

Each year, the NCAA has reported revenues of over $1 billion, and the peripheral revenues generated by college sports constitute additional billions.[3] However, few college athletes reap financial rewards. Some critics feel that this is unfair and exploitative, and one of the biggest debates in the world of college athletics concerns whether or not athletes should be paid. Critics say that this would make college sports a profession, rather than part of an educational system, but proponents of paying athletes argue that the system as it exists allows the NCAA and institutions to exploit players, building wealth for investors and executives without compensating the players, many of whom come from impoverished backgrounds.[4]

Another reason that advocates are pushing for compensation for college athletes is the considerable risks that many college athletes face. Injuries and concussions remain common among college athletes and can have long-term or life-changing consequences. Compared to nonathlete students, college athletes are more likely to suffer long-term injuries to their limbs or backs, concussions, and many other types of overuse injuries. While most athletes recover from injuries, there are well-documented cases of former or current athletes suffering fatal or severe injuries. What's more, athletes must purchase their own medical insurance. This is another major debate in the college sports field, and some argue that the NCAA should offer free insurance and injury coverage paid for with the revenues earned through college sports competitions. Questions about insurance have resurged as COVID-19 imposed additional risks on collegiate athletes.[5]

Long-Term Challenges and New Challenges

Compensation, or lack thereof, is the biggest current issue in the world of collegiate sports, but there are many other long-term challenges and problems facing the industry. Many critics argue that racial prejudice continues to play a major role in collegiate sports, especially in the distribution of benefits through schools and the NCAA. For most of American history, athletes of color were denied access to collegiate sports, and the integration of college sports teams was, in many ways, exploitative. Among those advocating for compensation for college athletes, many cite the exploitation of minority players as one of the reasons that NCAA economic management is problematic. Many young players of color come from impoverished backgrounds, and the distribution of resources means that the resources tend to go primarily to white students and students in the upper classes. A 2020 survey released by ESPN showed that 76 percent of college coaches and 65 percent of athletes see racism as a continuing problem on college campuses, and even higher percentages see racism as an issue in the college sports industry as it exists.[6]

There is also a disparity of investment and support for women's sports across the board. Numerous studies and years of reports from athletes and coaches show that interest in college sports among women has increased markedly over the past half century. But the NCAA and colleges have continued to invest heavily in male-dominated sports, with a far lower level of investment in women's sports. It has been argued that this is because audiences are more interested in men's sports, but this argument is problematic given that audience attraction is not supposed to be among the priorities of collegiate sports organizations. Further, many critics have argued that there is a substantial audience for women's sports that has gone largely untapped because media outlets, the NCAA, and colleges fail to market and emphasize their women's sports programs. With women increasing their share of the sports and fitness market nationwide, many critics have argued that organizations and the media need to devote more time and attention to this side of the college sports industry.[7]

Encouraging diversity can also be seen in the debate over the participation of trans athletes, which centers around whether they should be allowed to compete on teams aligning with their chosen gender or teams aligning with their biological sex.

The issue has divided Americans on many levels because there are concerns about fairness and equity to be considered, both with regard to the way that trans athletes are portrayed, treated, and made to feel accepted, and with the way that traditional leagues and teams have been constituted along perceived gender lines. The discussion on this issue is causing Americans to rethink some of the fundamental traditions in modern sports.

The Future of Sport

There is another major direction of change that is forcing Americans to reconsider definitions of competitive athletics. Esports, or "electronic sports," are based on participating in virtual digital contests. More than simply professional gaming, esports is a diverse and rapidly developing field that has dedicated competitors, investors, and fans around the world. It is creating an entirely new dimension to collegiate sports. The esports era has been developing for some time. In the 1980s, innovative video gamers first created the potential for player-versus-player (PVP) competition in digital environments. In the decades since, game designers have capitalized on wireless networks and internet technology, in conjunction with cutting-edge digital design and art, to create digital platforms where players can test their skills against other players virtually anywhere in the world. In the 2010s multiplayer online gaming reached a new zenith, and streaming platforms began broadcasting games. Some players began streaming their own content, in the process creating a new career, a "streamer," in which an individual earns revenues from sponsorships and advertising features. It soon became clear that gamers were drawing in massive audiences, and potentially massive revenues from sponsors and advertisers.

The draw of competitive gaming eventually helped foster the idea that it might be considered something similar to games like chess or checkers, strategic games that test hand-eye coordination, intelligence, strategic ability, and other characteristics.

Works Used

Adelson, Andrea. "Survey: Coaches, Athletes Think Racism Is an Issue." *ESPN.* Oct 14, 2020. https://www.espn.com/college-sports/story/_/id/30116337/coaches-athletes-feel-need-act-racism. Accessed 27 May 2021.

Berkowitz, Steve. "NCAA Reports Revenues of More Than $1 Billion in 2017." *USA Today.* Mar 7, 2018. https://www.usatoday.com/story/sports/college/2018/03/07/ncaa-reports-revenues-more-than-1-billion-2017/402486002/. Accessed 27 May 2021.

Berkowitz, Steve, Lindsay Schnell, and Dan Wolken. "'I Assumed They Were Treating Us Fairly': Why Can't NCAA Get Women's Basketball Right?" *USA Sports.* Mar 27, 2021. https://www.usatoday.com/in-depth/sports/ncaaw/2021/03/27/march-madness-why-cant-ncaa-get-womens-basketball-right/7012017002/. Accessed 27 May 2021.

Harlan, Jessica. "Lasting Benefits of College Sports for Student Athletes." *Gallup.*

Jun 24, 2020. https://news.gallup.com/opinion/gallup/313025/lasting-benefits-college-sports-student-athletes.aspx. Accessed 27 May 2021.

Illing, Sean. "College Football Is a Moneymaking Sham." *Vox*. Sep 5, 2017. https://www.vox.com/conversations/2017/9/5/16180862/college-football-ncaa-student-athlete-mike-mcintire. Accessed 27 May 2021.

Slama, Remington. "College Sports, Enter at Your Own Risk: An Overview of the NCAA Insurance Policies Available to its Student-Athletes." *Law Review*. Apr 20, 2021. https://lawreview.unl.edu/college-sports-enter-your-own-risk-overview-ncaa-insurance-policies-available-its-student-athletes. Accessed 27 May 2021.

Streeter, Kurt. "College Sports Can Be Exploitative: They Can Also Be a Lifeline." *The New York Times*. Mar 8, 2021. https://www.nytimes.com/2021/03/08/sports/ncaabasketball/athletes-pay-college.html. Accessed 27 May 2021.

1
Educational Environments

Photo of Faurot Field by Clare Murphy/KOMU, via Wikimedia.

The University of Missouri was sanctioned by the NCAA in 2018 for academic fraud after a tutor admitted to performing academic work for a dozen student athletes.

Balancing Sports and Studies for College Athletes

Since the beginning of college sports, there has been a debate over how to best balance the academic and athletic goals of educational institutions. Collegiate athletics is a multibillion-dollar industry that provides colleges and universities with millions in funding for student services, staff, and academic interests. But critics have also accused the collegiate sports industry of exploiting students and their families. Decades of reforms have been aimed at supporting the educational welfare of college athletes, who must balance academic achievement against both the desire to play and the economic pressures that drive the college sports industry.

What Do Sports Do for American Higher Education?

Writing about collegiate athletics in a 1970 article in the *American Quarterly*, Guy Lewis argued, "In many ways, sport contributed to the destruction of the isolated academic world and helped to make the nation more conscious of its colleges."[1] The introduction of organized college sports helped to create a sense of ownership among state residents, who could feel a sense of pride in their state's college teams. Prior to this era, colleges and universities were set apart from the general public. Increased public interest in the performance of colleges then helped generate revenues for colleges and universities to use on other projects and encouraged citizens to consider donating or otherwise supporting their local educational institutions.

According to sports historians, organized collegiate sports grew out of an effort to redirect the aggression of college-age men. In the early days of American higher education, colleges could be rough places. Each year, incoming freshmen were violently "hazed" by sophomores in a tradition that came to be called the "rush," and student attacks on faculty were common enough that the phenomenon was well known in pre–Civil War America. A number of universities tried to curb violent behavior by engaging students in manual labor, but this did little to solve the problem. A solution was found by engaging students in the same kinds of games and contests students organized in their free time. During the annual rushes, students often took part in informal football matches. In the decades leading up to the Civil War, a number of colleges and universities established organized contests between students. Boxing and rowing were among the first organized sports introduced at the Ivy Leagues, but many popular American sports were later added to the college and university athletic programs. College baseball games began in 1859, while football got its start with the establishment of the first collegiate football association (which included only Harvard, Yale, and Princeton) in 1872.[2]

Around the same time that the first collegiate sports were in development, universities and colleges also added physical education to the basic curriculum. Gymnasiums were built to accommodate classes and doubled as arenas for college sports teams to practice. Over time, college administrators and the public came to embrace physical education and collegiate sport as an important part of higher education. It was and is still frequently argued that physical education and participation in sport offers important lessons in cooperation, overcoming adversity, and teamwork while also improving students' physical skills, coordination, and health. Whereas sport had once been considered an activity primarily for the lower classes, participation in certain sports was incorporated into elite culture as well, and the contests between universities provided another dimension of collegiate allegiance among students, their families, and other local. Though the college sports industry has frequently been the target of criticism, numerous studies have shown that college athletes retain important life lessons that can, in some situations, assist in their later careers and in achieving other life goals.

The Scholarship Debate

In the late 1800s, colleges began recruiting students on the basis of athletic skill; this was the beginning of the "athletic scholarship" system in which colleges and universities subsidize educational fees for talented athletes. After the establishment of the National Collegiate Athletic Association (NCAA) in 1906, it became more common for universities to offer support and incentives to student athletes in order to recruit them for their sports programs. Competition between schools led to an escalating scholarship war, and there are many documented instances of universities and colleges engaging in unethical and perhaps illegal practices in order to attract top athletes. Eventually, the NCAA and state politicians attempted to regulate the college athletics system, in part to put an end to corruption and other unethical practices.[3] Though there were a number of movements to regulate collegiate athletics and the scholarship system, athletic scholarships remain a multibillion-dollar industry in the United States. In the 2019–2020 school year, for instance, colleges and universities invested more than $4 billion in athletic scholarship awards.[4]

One of the primary concerns among critics of athletic scholarships has been institutional exploitation. Critics argue that colleges and universities must also ensure that any student recruited as an athlete is also provided opportunities for education and other services to further academic achievement. As a result, the NCAA requires that any athlete playing collegiate sports must be an active student in good standing. A number of colleges and universities further limit a student's ability to participate in athletics unless the student maintains a certain level of academic performance. These measures are meant to protect the welfare of student athletes, most of whom will not achieve work as professional athletes after leaving higher education. The basic idea is to ensure that educational institutions investing in student athletes also emphasize academic achievement and career preparation.

Many of the scholarships offered to student athletes in the 2020s are offered through the NCAA, which has annual revenues of some $1 billion, most of which

($840 million) comes from revenues accrued through collegiate basketball. The NCAA is a non-profit organization, and allocates 90 percent of institutional income for scholarships, academic services for students, compliance investigations, and drug testing. This means that there are tens of millions in funds available for colleges and universities to use in recruiting players, and since the early 1900s educational institutions have been competing for NCAA and state and private funding.[5]

Academic Fraud and Academic Balance

For universities and colleges, athletic program success is closely linked to revenues, as successful athletic programs attract additional donations and investment and attract more students. Colleges and universities profit from athletic contests through television and streaming revenues, through patronage, and through city or state investment. With collegiate sports developing into a multibillion-dollar industry, universities and colleges have become even more dependent on this source of income.

Competition between athletics programs has led to a number of problems that have been the target of reformers, but one of the most pressing is academic fraud—when students, teachers, or administrators unethically provide a college athlete with academic advantages to protect his or her ability to participate in athletics. An educator issuing a passing grade to a student athlete who has failed a course is an example of academic fraud. There have been numerous sports scandals in which academic institutions were charged with falsifying test results or otherwise aiding students in cheating to maintain a certain level of academic performance.

Critics have argued that few students can successfully manage academic demands while playing high-level collegiate sports, but there have been few proposals for how to create a better balance between athletic and academic demands. Studies have shown that the amount of time needed to maintain peak athletic performance is difficult if not impossible to maintain for many students. Even for those who manage to maintain both academic and athletic performance, there may be a high cost in terms of work-life balance, and the pressure on student athletes constitutes a dangerous stressor with potential impacts on health and well-being.

Works Used

"Average per Athlete 2020." *Scholarship Stats.* 2021. https://scholarshipstats.com/average-per-athlete. Accessed 15 May 2021.

Drozdowski, Mark J. "Do Colleges Make Money from Athletics?" *Best Colleges.* Nov 16, 2020. https://www.bestcolleges.com/blog/do-college-sports-make-money/. Accessed 15 May 2021.

Guy, Lewis. "The Beginning of Organized Collegiate Sport." *American Quarterly.* Vol. 22, No. 2 (Summer, 1970).

Smith, Rodney K. "A Brief History of the National Collegiate Athletic Association's Role in Regulating Intercollegiate Athletics." *Marquette Sports Law Review.* Vol 11, No. 1 (2000).

Vanover, Eric T., and Michael M. DeBowes. "The Impact of Intercollegiate Athletics in Higher Education." *Academic Perspectives in Higher Education.* 2013. https://www.odu.edu/content/dam/odu/col-dept/efl/docs/intercollegiate-athletics-in-higher-education.pdf. Accessed 15 May 2021.

Notes

1. Lewis, "The Beginning of Organized Collegiate Sport."
2. Vanover and DeBowes, "The Impact of Intercollegiate Athletics in Higher Education).
3. Smith, "A Brief History of the National Collegiate Athletic Association's Role in Regulating Intercollegiate Athletics."
4. "Average per Athlete 2020," *Scholarship Stats.*
5. Drozdowski, "Do Colleges Make Money from Athletics?"

For College Athletes, Concern about Balancing Sports, Academics

By Bryan Toporek
EdWeek, April 28, 2015

The average student-athlete in the Pac-12 Conference logs roughly 50 hours per week on athletics during their respective sport's season, which often adversely affects their academic work, according to a new report commissioned by the conference.

The report, which *CBS Sports'* Dennis Dodd obtained (it has not been released publicly), surveyed 409 student-athletes from nine Pac-12 universities—excluding the University of Utah, the University of Arizona, and the University of Southern California—about their time demands from athletics. At least one athlete from each Pac-12 sport was included, and the respondent pool was split 50-50 by gender. Their answers revealed a number of troubling findings about student-athletes' academics-athletics balance, raising the specter of possible reforms in the years ahead.

Currently, the NCAA has a 20-hour limit on required athletic activities on a weekly basis; however, the average Pac-12 athlete reported spending 21 hours a week on such activities. They also claimed to spend an additional 29 hours on other athletic-related things such as voluntary activities, receiving treatment and traveling for competitions, which don't count under the current NCAA limit.

Four in five Pac-12 athletes reported having missed a class for competition during the 2014-15 academic year, and 54 percent said they did not have enough time to study for tests. "When asked how the athletic season affects their ability to focus on academics, students say they are too exhausted to study effectively, that they are unable to devote enough time to both their academics and tests, and that athletic stress negatively impacts their academic focus," the report says.

Former Northwestern quarterback Kain Colter, who's helping lead a unionization effort for collegiate student-athletes, testified last year about having to log 50- to 60-hour weeks during training camp on athletics. That commitment prevented him from pursuing certain academic interests, such as attempting to attend medical school or studying abroad, he testified during a National Labor Relations Board unionization hearing.

The idea of a "voluntary athletic activity" appears to be a misnomer for a large percentage of Pac-12 student-athletes, too. Nearly 3 in 4 (73 percent) said that team-based voluntary activities were effectively required, and many felt more pressured from coaches than team-mates to attend such activities. Some reported coaches taking attendance at voluntary practices, threatening to kick athletes off the team for missing voluntary activi-

Four in five Pac-12 athletes reported having missed a class for competition during the 2014–15 academic year, and 54 percent said they did not have enough time to study for tests.

ties, or punishing the entire team when athletes miss voluntary activities. Sixty-two percent of respondents said making said activities truly voluntary would improve their student-athlete experience.

Having such vast time commitments drastically reduces student-athletes' opportunity to sleep, the report found. Seventy-one percent of athletes said sleep is the top thing their athletic commitments prevented them from doing, while 55 percent said if they had an extra hour in their day, they would dedicate it to sleep. "Many say they would use a hypothetical 2- to 3-week break to sleep and physically rest as their bodies and minds are exhausted from the non-stop stress during the competitive season," the report found.

Beyond making voluntary activities truly voluntary, student-athletes wanted to see non-practice hours extended from 10 p.m. to 6 a.m., giving them more time to complete their academic commitments and sleep. They would also like their schools to make it easier on them to find part-time jobs, as their athletic time commitments largely limit them from doing so at the moment.

Whether these findings spark any major reforms remains uncertain at the moment.

"The thing that's unclear right now is whether that will lead to [NCAA] legislation," Pac-12 commissioner Larry Scott told *CBS Sports*.

"The main takeaway is—in general—student-athletes are very, very satisfied with their experience," he added. "They're pushed for sure, challenged. Sometimes [they] feel like it's too much."

Print Citations

CMS: Toporek, Bryan. "For College Athletes, Concern about Balancing Sports, Academics." In *The Reference Shelf: College Sports,* edited by Micah L. Issitt, 7-8. Amenia, NY: Grey House Publishing, 2021.

MLA: Toporek, Bryan. "For College Athletes, Concern about Balancing Sports, Academics." *The Reference Shelf: College Sports,* edited by Micah L. Issitt, Grey Publishing, 2021, pp. 7-8. House

APA: Toporek, B. (2021). For college athletes, concern about balancing sports, academics. In Micah L. Issitt (Ed.), *The reference shelf: College sports* (pp. 7-8). Amenia, NY: Grey House Publishing.

In Scandal After Scandal, NCAA Takes Fall for Complicit Colleges

By Rick Eckstein

The Conversation, November 1, 2017

College sports fans probably weren't surprised to learn that the University of North Carolina (UNC) had been engaged in academic fraud for decades. In this particular instance, students, predominately varsity athletes, were enrolled in classes with few (if any) academic requirements. They almost always received high grades.

The UNC scandal is just one of many recent examples where universities have prioritized athletic prowess over academic integrity.

And where was the National Collegiate Athletic Association (NCAA) in all this? Amazingly, it essentially shrugged off the apparent transgressions, even after UNC admitted to them. Is the NCAA abdicating its oversight responsibilities?

Critics of the NCAA, such as *Bloomberg News'* Joe Nocera, have long argued that the organization has zero credibility as a regulator of college sports. Nocera and others tend to view the NCAA as either hypocritical or corrupt.

But without appearing sympathetic to the NCAA, I believe it is not the prime offender in the UNC case. It is simply doing the bidding of a higher education system that has gone off the academic rails. If the NCAA is Oz's projection on the wall, a profit-oriented higher education system is behind the curtain pulling the levers.

The Athletic Arms Race

In my recent book, I link higher education's misplaced priorities to the explosion of costs associated with intercollegiate athletics and youth sports.

This research, along with studies by the Knight Commission, the Drake Group and the Association of Research Libraries, shows that university spending on intercollegiate sports has vastly outpaced spending on instruction and research over the past two decades.

This spending spree has led to an arms race, or what sports sociologist Howard Nixon II calls an "athletic trap" that ensnares universities in incessant funding of high-visibility sports programs.

Contrary to popular belief, very few college sports programs operate in the black. According to data from the NCAA and U.S. Department of Education, fewer than 25 of the more than 300 NCAA Division I programs earn more than they spend.

Athletic department deficits at some schools run upwards of US$20 million per year.

Whenever athletic expenses exceed revenues, schools must make up the gap through other means.

At state schools, this could include more public funding, although that is becoming quite rare. More likely, schools will try to address the deficit through increasing tuition, implementing generic "student fees" or soliciting alumni for more money.

Paying for What, Exactly?

On the surface, none of this seems logical. Why pour so many resources into athletic programs? If students end up bearing the financial burden and education programs suffer, where is the return on the investment?

More than 100 years ago, sociologist Thorstein Veblen first identified the "corporatization" of higher education, with university presidents as "captains of solvency" who focus their energies on "principles of spectacular publicity" that will impress current and future donors.

Not much has changed in the last century. Higher education has become more about cultivating a school's "brand" than cultivating critical thinkers, more about alumni checkbooks than about student notebooks. Is it any wonder that college presidents are increasingly referred to as CEOs and are being recruited from the corporate world?

If we think about college sports as a marketing venture rather than an educational venture, all of this spending makes perfect sense. Think of players as walking advertisements—each branded with the school's logo—who appear before millions of viewers on ESPN and ABC.

Large schools are especially concerned with brand development and revenue streams, which come from a combination of dedicated alumni, fans and corporate sponsors.

Meanwhile, smaller Division I schools and Division III schools use athletics not just for brand recognition but to manipulate their enrollment statistics and improve their "selectivity index."

Generally, varsity athletes are admitted through an early decision process that operates somewhat independently from the regular admissions process. But only the regular process figures into calculations of a college's acceptance rates. Athletes who are admitted early reduce the number of acceptances offered to the regular applicant pool.

This lowers the school's acceptance rate and raises its perceived selectivity—all without any substantive educational improvements.

Like their Division I counterparts, Division III schools also believe that visible and successful sports programs will spawn increased alumni contributions. The supporting data for this, however, are mixed. Most schools end up treading water (or slowly sinking) as increased spending doesn't keep pace with increases in alumni contributions.

The Empty "Student-Athlete" Slogan

Officially born in 1910, the NCAA has always had trouble balancing its dual mission of promoting and regulating intercollegiate sports. Part of this promotion has been cultivating the "amateur" status of college sports, and how it is "purer" than commercialized professional sports.

Nothing represents that marketing scheme better than the "student-athlete" concept.

Former NCAA president Walter Byers first coined the term in the 1950s while fighting a worker's compensation claim by the widow of a college football player who had died during a game. "Student-athlete" has since becoming something of a mantra among those who work at any level within intercollegiate sports.

> **University spending on intercollegiate sports has vastly outpaced spending on instruction and research over the past two decades.**

As a result, the NCAA postures as a de facto defender of academic integrity, even while its bylaws state otherwise. Rules approved by the NCAA in 2016 state that colleges should set their own academic integrity standards, with the NCAA intervening only when those internal rules are violated.

In the UNC case, the NCAA is refusing to second-guess the school's determination that no internal rules have been violated, despite what appears to be serious academic misconduct.

Following the NCAA's statutory logic, universities would crack down on athletics-centered academic fraud if they really wanted to. Instead, as my research and the work of others show, schools have become organizationally and ideologically addicted to intercollegiate sports.

Universities are convinced that they only need one more "fix" to reach intercollegiate sports nirvana: just one more new facility, one more high-profile coach, one more no-work course and one more entertainment complex to attract top recruits. But the athletics arms race keeps spiraling, and higher education keeps moving farther away from its educational mission.

The NCAA is a convenient scapegoat, but the problem lies much deeper. Is "college education" itself becoming an oxymoron? Was long-time college sports critic Murray Sperber correct when he said that universities were more about "beer and circuses" than about teaching and research?

Perhaps Thorstein Veblen was also right when he originally subtitled his book on higher education "A Study in Total Depravity."

Print Citations

CMS: Eckstein, Rick. "In Scandal After Scandal, NCAA Takes Fall for Complicit Colleges." In *The Reference Shelf: College Sports,* edited by Micah L. Issitt, 9-12. Amenia, NY: Grey House Publishing, 2021.

MLA: Eckstein, Rick. "In Scandal After Scandal, NCAA Takes Fall for Complicit Colleges." *The Reference Shelf: College Sports,* edited by Micah L. Issitt, Grey House Publishing, 2021, pp. 9-12.

APA: Eckstein, R. (2021). In scandal after scandal, NCAA takes fall for complicit colleges. In Micah L. Issitt (Ed.), *The reference shelf: College sports* (pp. 9-12). Amenia, NY: Grey House Publishing

An "Epidemic" of Academic Fraud

By Jake New

Inside Higher Ed, July 8, 2016

The National Collegiate Athletic Association announced Thursday that it had placed Georgia Southern University on two years' probation after finding that two former staff members committed academic fraud for three football players.

In a statement Thursday, the university noted that the violations were self-reported and that Georgia Southern self-imposed most of the resulting penalties. "Institutional checks and balances promptly detected the actions of these rogue former employees, despite their efforts to hide what they knew to be policy violations," the university stated.

While it's common for institutions to place the blame on a few "rogue former employees," the case at Georgia Southern is only the most recent example of what critics and other observers of big-time college sports call an epidemic of academic fraud. In the last two years, more than a half dozen NCAA institutions have committed academic misconduct, and the association says it is investigating another 20 for similar violations.

An analysis by *Inside Higher Ed* of the association's major infraction database found that the NCAA has punished Division I institutions at least 15 times for academic fraud in the last decade.

"It's an epidemic and a problem that will continue until faculty take control of their campuses," said David Ridpath, a professor of sports administration at Ohio University and an advocate for reforming the academic side of college sports. "This can be changed, but we simply have to want to do it. This will not stop until we define what we are: professional sports being played in the higher ed space or a cocurricular activity played by students?"

Earlier this year, the NCAA's Division I Council adopted new rules designed to update its academic integrity policies for the first time since 1983.

Colleges must now "maintain and adhere to written academic integrity policies that apply to the entire student body." If a college breaks its own rules, the NCAA would consider that to be a case of "academic misconduct." At the same time, the new rule redefines "impermissible academic assistance" as "academic conduct involving a staff member or booster that falls outside of a school's academic misconduct policies, provides a substantial impact on the student-athlete's eligibility and is not the type of academic assistance" generally available to all students.

"The legislation aims to strike an appropriate balance between a school administration's role in deciding academic integrity issues on campus and the NCAA's collective role in reinforcing and upholding the NCAA's core academic principles," the association said.

Two teams whose academic misconduct helped lead to the new guidelines met in this year's Final Four of the NCAA men's basketball tournament: the University of North Carolina at Chapel Hill and Syracuse University.

In 2005, following a season of poor academic performance from his players, Syracuse's head basketball coach, Jim Boeheim, hired a new director of basketball operations and gave him an imperative: "fix" the academic problems of his athletes. The new director's solution, according to the NCAA, was for athletics staff members to access and monitor the email accounts of several players, communicate directly with faculty members as if the staff members were the athletes and then complete course work for them. In one case, an athlete had his eligibility restored by turning in a paper to raise a grade he had earned the previous year.

The paper was written by the director and a basketball facility receptionist.

The fraud finally came to light last year after a lengthy series of investigations by the university and the NCAA. Syracuse self-imposed a postseason ban last year, and then the NCAA announced a number of sanctions against the university, including vacating more than 100 of Boeheim's wins and suspending him for nine conference games this past season.

The fraud at University of North Carolina lasted much longer. For 18 years, some employees at UNC Chapel Hill knowingly steered about 3,000 students—1,500 of them athletes—toward "paper courses" that never met, were not taught by any faculty members and in which the only work required was a single research paper that received a high grade no matter the content.

Roy Williams, the men's basketball coach, maintains he was not aware of the fraud. "We had a problem," Williams said ahead of the Final Four game. "We're embarrassed, we're mad, we're ticked off about what happened. We know men's basketball had nothing to do with it and we're very proud about that."

Yet the majority of those in the know were academic advisers to men's basketball and football players, the latter group of which made up more than half of the athletes taking the courses, according to a report the university released in 2014. In television interviews that year, a former player under Williams—a member of his 2005 championship team—said players enrolled in the paper courses and that the head coach was aware of the fraud.

That year, when the team won the NCAA tournament, UNC men's basketball players accounted for at least 35 enrollments in the phony courses, according to the university. Over all, men's basketball players accounted for more than 12 percent of all athletes taking the courses. The NCAA is still mulling how to punish the university.

The association's Division I Committee on Infractions has had its hands full in the last year dealing with other recent cases of fraud.

In June 2013, a former assistant men's basketball coach at Southern Methodist

University determined that an athlete he recruited to the team needed to take a summer course to meet NCAA eligibility standards. The assistant coach met with the athlete and his mother and encouraged the incoming freshman to enroll in an online course. Soon after the athlete enrolled in the online course, he met an administrative assistant in the men's basketball office, who "took an interest in his life and academic work," according to the NCAA's report. In July 2014, the assistant obtained the athlete's username and password for his online summer course, as well as for his email account.

She completed all of the athlete's assignments and exams, earning him an A-minus grade. Last year, the NCAA placed Southern Methodist's basketball program on three-year probation and banned the team from postseason play as punishment.

Online courses were also at the center of academic fraud found by the NCAA at Weber State University in late 2014. A year earlier, a math instructor began completing course work for five football players—including tests, quizzes and a final exam—by logging in to the athletes' profiles in an online math course.

In the most recent case at Georgia Southern, according to the NCAA, a former assistant compliance director gave an athlete a flash drive containing her work from when she was enrolled in the same course. The athlete later pulled an assignment from the flash drive and submitted the work as if it were his own.

A former assistant director of student-athlete services at the university also wrote and submitted 10 extra credit assignments for two football players. She obtained the players' log-in information and submitted the assignments without the athletes' knowledge. The players still failed those courses. Georgia Southern faced a similar scandal in 2010, when a former assistant coach and director of men's basketball operations completed course work for two basketball players. The fraud included writing essays, taking tests and participating in required online chats for the athletes.

In the NCAA report released Thursday, the Committee on Infractions noted that since 2014, at least three institutions have violated NCAA rules when an institutional staff member performed academic work for a current or incoming athlete. When asked if the association was concerned by the large number of fraud cases in recent years, Greg Sankey, chair of the NCAA's Division I Committee on Infractions and commissioner of the Southeastern Conference, pointed reporters to that section of the report.

> **It's up to colleges to make sure that an increasing pressure to succeed both on the field and in the classroom does not create the kind of employees who are desperate enough to resort to fraud.**

"Whether one quantifies the number of cases as simply the three listed, plus the one today, or by identifying others, I think I can say on behalf of the committee that every one of these cases is troubling," Sankey said. "We have high expectations, and those are noted in this report and in others, and people in leadership roles need to fulfill those obligations."

The three institutions mentioned in the report include Southern Methodist, Weber State and the University of Southern Mississippi.

The NCAA determined earlier this year that Southern Mississippi had committed academic fraud. For two years, the former head men's basketball coach directed his staff to travel to where prospective athletes lived so they could assist the players with their course work. The recruits, all students at two-year institutions, were struggling to earn the necessary academic credentials to transfer to Southern Mississippi and be immediately eligible to compete.

According to the NCAA, the assistants completed numerous assignments in several online courses for seven athletes. In one case, a recruit was such a weak student that his coach described him as "as far away from graduating as any kid I've ever had." Yet when he took three online courses through another institution to become eligible at Southern Mississippi, his GPA for those courses was 3.75. According to the NCAA, one of the graduate assistants completed at least 20 math assignments in those courses.

In September 2013, the former head men's basketball coach learned that a recruit needed two English courses and a math course in order to be eligible, but the student could not pay for them. The coach went to a pharmacy and purchased four prepaid $500 credit cards. He gave the cards to his graduate assistants, who then used them to pay the registration fees of the online courses. One of the graduate assistants completed 75 of the athlete's online English assignments. The recruit later admitted that he did not register, pay for or complete any of the online courses.

That the fraud involved students who were not yet enrolled in the university and courses not offered at the institution demonstrated how the pressures of big-time college athletics can breed academic impropriety far beyond the walls of the offending campus. Three months earlier, the NCAA concluded that a former assistant football coach at the University of Louisiana at Lafayette had made arrangements with the head of a Mississippi testing center to falsify the ACT scores of players and recruits.

"This thing has tentacles," Ridpath, of Ohio University, said at the time. "That's been proven over and over again. High schools, testing sites, junior colleges—the corruption trickles down from the universities and affects all levels of education."

In May, the University of Mississippi announced that the same assistant coach had pulled the same scam when he was an assistant coach for Mississippi's football team in 2010. In addition, the university said that an assistant women's basketball coach and the women's basketball director of operations signed up for several online courses on behalf of two prospective players who were still enrolled at two-year institutions. The pair paid for the courses and completed homework assignments, papers, quizzes and exams for the recruits.

Amy Perko, executive director of the Knight Commission on Intercollegiate Athletics, said it's up to colleges to make sure that an increasing pressure to succeed both on the field and in the classroom does not create the kind of employees who are desperate enough to resort to fraud.

"The uptick in academic fraud cases underscores the importance of creating a culture of academic integrity for the entire athletics program," Perko said.

Print Citations

CMS: New, Jake. "An 'Epidemic' of Academic Fraud." In *The Reference Shelf: College Sports,* edited by Micah L. Issitt, 13-17. Amenia, NY: Grey House Publishing, 2021.

MLA: New, Jake. "An 'Epidemic' of Academic Fraud." *The Reference Shelf: College Sports,* edited by Micah L. Issitt, Grey House Publishing, 2021, pp. 13-17.

APA: New, J. (2021). An "epidemic" of academic fraud. In Micah L. Issitt (Ed.), *The reference shelf: College sports* (pp. 13-17). Amenia, NY: Grey House Publishing.

Like College Athletes, These High School Players Get an Assist on Academics

By Stephen Sawchuck
EdWeek, **February 21, 2020**

Cincinnati high school math teacher Jill Ruby is a second coach of sorts for a group of students who are already answerable to the adults who school them on the techniques, rules, and strategies of the sport they play.

At Hughes STEM High School, she has a caseload of about 30 athletes whose grades and attendance patterns she checks on a weekly basis. If any of them have an F or two D-level grades, she devises a plan with them to pull up those marks—including attending after-school study sessions, prompting them to communicate with their teachers about making up missed work, or putting them in touch with someone who can tutor them on a tough literature concept.

In her coaching role, Ruby has helped students apply for colleges and even fill out the FAFSA.

"It has been the highlight of my year so far, getting to connect with kids and getting them to grow academically and persevere through the struggles they've been having," Ruby said.

Each of the Cincinnati district's 14 high schools with athletic departments now has a teacher, administrator, or counselor who serves in a role similar to Ruby's. The program, in effect, offers for secondary students the same type of developmental support common for college athletes who must meet eligibility requirements to play.

"We've got a lot of students in the district that are battling different things on a daily basis, and the support they need sometimes is just one more person that's really there to care for them, support them, hear them out," said Joshua Hardin, the athletics manager for the 36,000-student Cincinnati district. "Athletics is a way for a lot of students in the district to be connected to the school and community and to feel like they have an opportunity to have their thing."

"No Pass, No Play"

Now in its second full year in the Cincinnati district, the program, dubbed the Academic and Athletic Accountability Pathway, is an extra layer of support for students whose prowess on the athletic field tends to get a brighter spotlight than their academics. In addition to the personalized support, students who play sports in the

Queen City get a free boot camp to prep for the ACT. The program is a new wrinkle on what's now an established part of secondary sports—eligibility.

In 1984, Texas instituted the first so-called "no pass, no play" rule, which requires students to pass all their courses to participate in sports or extracurricular activities. Some 30-odd states followed with variations of their own—often, as in Ohio, leaving it up to local districts to specify the academic measure and penalties. Some districts work attendance or conduct into the calculus in addition to a grade or course-completion measure. The penalties for missing the cutoffs range from being benched for a couple of weeks through several semesters.

Research generally suggests that no-pass-no-play policies do shape students' attendance patterns and grades.

Further complicating matters, state high school athletic associations also set benchmarks that can effectively carry the same weight as state law. That's the case in Ohio, where the Ohio High School Athletic Association requires high school students to carry and pass five one-credit courses. Many Ohio districts have interpreted that as at least a D or 1.0 GPA.

Research generally suggests that no-pass-no-play policies do shape students' attendance patterns and grades.

"There is no doubt about the fact that if you require students to be eligible to play on a team, they are more serious about their studies; there is no doubt about the fact that they are more motivated," said Angela Lumpkin, a professor in the department of kinesiology and sports management at Texas Tech University, in Lubbock. "If you have to pass your algebra class to play on a football team, you'll find a way to pass your algebra class."

But it's far less clear exactly how stringent the standard should be. Does too low send a bad signal about the relative value of academics? Does too high encourage cheating or push students who mainly attend school for athletics out the door?

Such questions are topics of perennial debate, and as a result, any movement in districts' eligibility standards attracts scrutiny. (Both the Dayton and the Stow-Munroe Falls districts in Ohio kicked up controversy in recent years when they proposed lowering their eligibility GPAs.)

Building Supports

Cincinnati, like many other Ohio districts, had tried to strike a balance between too high and too low. The school board had set the bar higher than many districts at 2.0—a C average. And though it had established free tutoring tables after school for students needing more attention, what was missing was some coherent system for motivating students to pull up weak grades.

When Hardin, the district's athletics manager, started looking at achievement data among athletes, he found some troubling patterns. Most of his athletes cleared the 1.0 GPA bar, but fewer were meeting the 2.0 mark. That wasn't just academically troubling news for players with college aspirations—it also meant that those vying for athletic scholarships could be in for a rude awakening. The National Collegiate Athletic Association requires at least a 2.3 GPA for Division I athletes and a 2.2 for Division II.

For the pilot year, in 2018-19, Hardin cobbled together funding to select and pay the AAA Pathway coaches a stipend similar to the ones that athletic coaches were receiving. And he brought on Stephanie Price, who had worked in athletic development at the University of Northern Kentucky, to design a training manual for the course and run the program. Price meets with each coach twice each quarter, offering assistance in how they can support each of their charges.

Ruby, only in her second year of teaching, had already found out that attending her students' games helped her build relationships with them. Now, as an AAA Pathway coach, she has another way to connect. A lot of what she does is more like counseling, she said, trying to empower students to address the root of a low grade—for instance, how to tell a teacher that they didn't understand something and need extra help.

"You can see a kid walk out [of our meetings] almost standing a bit taller and thinking, 'OK, I can have an adult conversation and something good can come out of it,' " she said.

And although other districts also offer help for athletes, "I feel like the consistency is really big in what makes this program different," Ruby said.

For all that, the basic idea of supports for athletes does pull from a higher education model that's had its share of scandal—most notably in 2014 at the University of North Carolina at Chapel Hill. Independent reports there found athletes were enrolled in allegedly fake "paper" classes to maintain their eligibility.

But Jerry Butler, an 8th grade social studies teacher at Shroder High School, thinks the opposite is true in Cincinnati's version. Before AAA Pathways, he said, when grade checks were done quarterly, a student could play nearly 10 weeks of football before anyone checked his or her grades. And athletic coaches and building athletic directors held all the cards.

"It was like the Wild, Wild West—basically anything went," said Butler, a 27-year veteran and former athletic coach. "You need an extra set of eyes to just hold everyone accountable."

Under AAA Pathway, Butler said, he's even pulled rank on athletic coaches, demanding that a student sit for a study session instead of going to practice. And students know they have to care about their schoolwork if only because a low score means Butler will be coming to check on them.

"It's good for me, because at times I do slip on my work," said Tommy Young, a sophomore Butler coaches at Shroder High who wrestles and plays football.

Tommie Steed III, a sophomore at Woodward Career & Technical High School is aiming high. While he'd like to win a track and field scholarship to college, he says his goal this year is to get a 4.0 in his academic classes.

"I don't think people understand the way we have to balance sports and education," he said. "It affects your grades, and your grade is what is going to get you into college, not sports."

Slippery Slope?

The program clocks in at about $100,000 for 2019-20, not extravagant but also not nothing at a time of tight school budgets. But the school board and other departments have been generally supportive.

"We do at times hear comments in response to other clubs—arts and music—and my response is always, I support extracurriculars for the district as a whole," said Hardin, adding that he's has been talking with his counterparts in those divisions about expanding the program to encompass them.

AAA Pathway is too new to have much data behind it, but Price, the program leader, ticks off some successes, including three students who were flagged for help through the program last school year and who this year qualified for Division II football scholarships in college. Coaches like Butler are integrating the support into other initiatives, including a social-emotional development program for boys.

"Anecdotally, we have AAA coaches who are in the second year who say the culture is changing. Student athletes are holding themselves accountable and others accountable," Price said. "And we're not losing kids to eligibility problems—especially early on."

As to whether such an approach could or should be replicated in other districts, Lumpkin is of two minds. She said she's for anything that supports students to do their best academically but not if districts start encouraging less rigorous coursework or cheating the way some colleges have.

Although there is far less money at stake in high school athletics than at the collegiate level, the outlays can still be considerable, she noted. (Some Texas districts have built high school football stadiums costing upwards of $70 million.)

"It's not that big in high schools, no, but that doesn't mean it won't be," Lumpkin said. "To me, one of the kind of revealing facts is that school districts have started calling them 'student athletes.' High school adolescents should be students, period, and they should have lots of opportunities for extracurriculars."

Print Citations

CMS: Sawchuck, Stephen. "Like College Athletes, These High School Players Get an Assist on Academics." In *The Reference Shelf: College Sports,* edited by Micah L. Issitt, 18-21. Amenia, NY: Grey House Publishing, 2021.

MLA: Sawchuck, Stephen. "Like College Athletes, These High School Players Get an Assist on Academics." *The Reference Shelf: College Sports,* edited by Micah L. Issitt, Grey House Publishing, 2021, pp. 18-21.

APA: Sawchuck, S. (2021). Like college athletes, these high school players get an assist on academics. In Micah L. Issitt (Ed.), *The reference shelf: College sports* (pp. 18-21). Amenia, NY: Grey House Publishing.

NCAA Punishes Missouri in Blatant Academic Fraud Case

By Doug Lederman
Inside Higher Ed, February 1, 2019

A former tutor at the University of Missouri at Columbia performed academic work—including taking three full online courses—for a dozen athletes, helping to keep many of them eligible to compete, the National Collegiate Athletic Association found Thursday.

The NCAA's Division I Committee on Infractions imposed a stinging set of penalties on the university, including a ban on postseason competition in football next season and in baseball and softball this spring and fines of 1 percent of the annual budgets in those sports. Missouri officials blasted the NCAA for what Chancellor Alexander Cartwright called its "harsh and inconsistent" decision, and vowed to appeal them.

The NCAA committee said the penalties could have been worse had the panel concluded that the tutor was acting either at the encouragement or with the knowledge of other university officials, as she asserted was the case.

The former mathematics tutor, Yolanda Kumar, whose November 2016 confession to Missouri administrators brought the case to the university's (and the NCAA's) attention, had asserted that athletics administrators pressured her to make sure her tutees passed, and that supervisors had "approved and rewarded her for her conduct," the NCAA wrote. (Kumar was not identified by name in the NCAA's infractions report, as is the association's custom. But she put herself into public view by taking to social media and, in 2017, offering to share confidential details about the case in exchange for $3,000 so she could pay a university debt and get her transcript from Missouri.)

"But the investigation did not support the allegation that her colleagues directed her to complete the work for the student-athletes," David M. Roberts, special adviser to the president of the University of Southern California and head of the NCAA panel that heard Missouri's case, said during a media call Thursday.

According to the NCAA report's findings, the tutor was told by an athletics department official in 2015 that a male basketball player "needed to pass" an applied statistics course over the summer to graduate. The tutor told the NCAA that she interpreted this interaction to mean that she should do whatever was needed to ensure the athlete's success, and that she "resorted to completing work" on his behalf.

She wound up, over the next 18 months, completing work for six athletes in University of Missouri math courses, including a self-paced online applied statistics course for which she completed and in some cases submitted assignments on the athletes' behalf.

She also helped athletes fulfill some of their university math requirements through online courses offered by other colleges, which the NCAA asserts that "a significant portion of the [Missouri] student population" does because "Missouri's math courses are historically difficult." (A university spokesman did not respond to requests for information about how commonly that actually happens.) The tutor completed course work for four athletes enrolled in an algebra class at a "local non-NCAA institution" that the report does not identify. Two other athletes took an online algebra course offered by Adams State University, in Colorado.

The NCAA concluded that the tutor had also helped two athletes score high enough on Missouri's (unproctored) math placement exam to place out of remedial math. They ended up playing for Missouri before ultimately being found guilty of cheating under the university's honor code.

As is true for just about every college sports case involving academic wrongdoing that has unfolded in the last few years, the NCAA's response to the Missouri situation brought repeated comparisons to the association's handling of the long-term academic wrongdoing at the University of North Carolina at Chapel Hill, which evaded NCAA penalties in 2017 in part because the

> **In the Missouri case, by contrast, the university "acknowledged that the tutor completed student-athletes' work and, in most instances, this conduct violated its honor code."**

university aggressively fought the charges and in part because the wrongdoing didn't technically violate the association's rules because the academic fraud also benefited hundreds of students who were not athletes.

Many commentators (especially sports columnists from nearby cities) struggled to reconcile UNC's escape from penalties with the harsh penalties imposed on Missouri (including fines of more than 1 percent of the annual budgets of the football, baseball and softball programs) for the actions of what many characterized as a "rogue" tutor.

"As it turns out, honesty isn't always the best policy," *The Athletic* said.

There is something to that critique, as the infractions panel indirectly acknowledges in its public report. Explaining why the Missouri and North Carolina cases are "distinguishable," the committee said that "UNC stood by the courses and the grades it awarded student-athletes," asserting that "although courses were created and graded by an office secretary, student-athletes completed their own work." In the Missouri case, by contrast, the university "acknowledged that the tutor completed student-athletes' work and, in most instances, this conduct violated its honor code."

While the infractions panel praised Missouri for its cooperation, and generally found its officials not to be culpable, the NCAA did not hold it blameless. "In the [committee's] past academic cases, [it] has consistently held both the institution and the institutional employee who engaged in the unethical conduct accountable for their actions," the panel's report said.

The potential penalties against Missouri were actually mitigated, the NCAA committee said, by the fact that the university disclosed the violations to the NCAA as soon as it learned of them. But institutions are also responsible for "self-detection" of violations, a responsibility the panel concluded Missouri did not fulfill. "The offending conduct continued for one year. But for the tutor's decision to come forward with her conduct, Missouri would not have known that the tutor was completing student-athletes' academic work," its report stated.

Missouri's explanation was that it has a "robust" program in place for educating its employees and a "culture of compliance" that encouraged the tutor to come forward. "Missouri is correct in that those are examples of well-functioning compliance systems," the panel wrote, but "its application to this case ... is a stretch. The record did not demonstrate that Missouri failed to monitor, but it also did not demonstrate that Missouri had systems in place designed for prompt self-detection associated with this mitigating factor (e.g., spot checking metadata on submitted assignments)."

In addition to the postseason bans and monetary fines, Missouri's football, softball and baseball teams face recruiting limitations and the vacation of victories in which the ineligible athletes competed.

Print Citations

CMS: Lederman, Doug. "NCAA Punishes Missouri in Blatant Academic Fraud Case." In *The Reference Shelf: College Sports,* edited by Micah L. Issitt, 22-24. Amenia, NY: Grey House Publishing, 2021.

MLA: Lederman, Doug. "NCAA Punishes Missouri in Blatant Academic Fraud Case." *The Reference Shelf: College Sports,* edited by Micah L. Issitt, Grey House Publishing, 2021, pp. 22-24.

APA: Lederman, D. (2021). NCAA punishes Missouri in blatant academic fraud case. In Micah L. Issitt (Ed.), *The reference shelf: College sports* (pp. 22-24). Amenia, NY: Grey House Publishing.

In College Sports, Non-Athletes Suffer Just as Much as the Stars on the Field

By Tom Joyce
The Guardian, October 16, 2019

In defiance of the NCAA, California governor Gavin Newsom signed SB 206 into law last month, better known as the Fair Pay to Play Act. Backed by Bernie Sanders and NBA superstar LeBron James, the bill allows college athletes in the state to profit from their image and likeness.

The bill comes one year after the NCAA, the largest governing body for college sports in the United States, reportedly amassed $1.1bn in revenue. Most of this money comes from the men's basketball March Madness tournament, according to CNBC, and a large portion also comes from college football bowl games. Although the Fair Pay to Play Act would not force the NCAA to pay athletes for any of those tournaments, it will allow them to do paid public appearances, sign endorsement deals, offer private lessons and sell their memorabilia.

The act is a sign of progress but it will only apply to a select few: while high-profile football and basketball players from successful programs are marketable, most student athletes are not famous enough to warrant endorsement deals or a market in signed memorabilia. However, when it comes to college athletics, there is a far larger issue that is being ignored: its actual price tag and who funds its existence.

The notion that all college sports teams across the United States are generating millions of dollars for their respective schools and every NCAA athlete is being exploited is unfounded. Except for some elite football and men's basketball programs, expenses tend to outstrip revenues, and the burden is largely placed on *nonathletes*, driving up the cost of their degrees.

The cost of college athletics varies greatly from school to school and oftentimes depends on which one of the three NCAA Divisions a school is in. The elite Division I teams (except for Ivy League schools) are allowed to offer full athletic scholarships to players, Division II teams primarily offer their athletes partial scholarships while Division III teams cannot offer athletic scholarships at all, according to *Prep Scholar*.

The NCAA reported in 2016 that the average Division I school lost $12.6m annually on athletics if they don't have a football team, and $14.4m if they do. In Division II, the annual loss per school as of 2014 was $5.1m if they had a football team and $4.1m if they did not. For Division III, football schools lost $3.1m on athletics while

Except for some elite football and men's basketball programs, expenses tend to outstrip revenues, and the burden is largely placed on nonathletes, driving up the cost of their degrees.

those without football experienced a $1.6m loss.

Largely, student fees and hiked tuition subsidize these costs at smaller private universities, although taxpayers contribute at state government-operated public colleges. Even so, a 2010 *Washington Post* report revealed that nine public colleges in Virginia charged each student more than $1,000 annually in fees to fund their athletic department.

The alternative to hiking fees is to cut sports teams entirely, which is exactly what Bacone College and Malone University have done in recent years.

Malone, a small private Christian school in Ohio with approximately 1,600 students, decided to cut the school's Division II football team to make additional funding available for academics. The school's official website reports they will save approximately $1m annually by cutting football. Recently, the school added cybersecurity and criminal and restorative justice programs.

Meanwhile, when Ferlin Clark became the president of Oklahoma's Bacone College in 2018, he cut his school's NAIA (a smaller NCAA alternative) football and rodeo programs to help erase $2m in debt and redirect funds towards the classroom.

Clark, who did not reply to requests from *The Guardian* for this story, explained his rationale to KTUL in 2018. "I think the core of it is we became a sports institute rather than an academic institution, and we had 16 athletic programs rather than 13 academic programs, so we needed to realign who we really are," he said.

Although financial woes forced Malone University and Bacone College to admit athletics drained resources, they are in the minority. At other schools like the University of Houston and UC Santa Cruz, students have voted in recent years in favor of increasing their own tuition fees to subsidize their athletic departments

Oftentimes, colleges mislead on the fiscal burden sports present because schools include subsidies to their athletic department as revenue on their financial reports. In 2018 *USA Today Sports* compiled financial reports from 230 public colleges' athletic departments and in their explanation of the revenue column, they noted student fees, tuition and state funds were being counted. On financial reports, this makes it appear as though the athletic departments are self-sufficient or even making money for their respective schools when they are not.

Still, college sports are not going away anytime soon. In 2019, there were five new college football programs established and in 2020, there will be four more, none of which will be Division I, according to *Next College Student Athlete*.

Even though elite college athletes could soon be profiting from their efforts, there is no foreseeable legislation to help out the millions of nonathlete students caught in this unrelated–yet far more prevalent–issue.

Print Citations

CMS: Joyce, T. "In College Sports, Non-Athletes Suffer Just as Much as the Stars on the Field." In *The Reference Shelf: College Sports,* edited by Micah L. Issitt, 25-27. Amenia, NY: Grey House Publishing, 2021.

MLA: Joyce, T. "In College Sports, Non-Athletes Suffer Just as Much as the Stars on the Field." *The Reference Shelf: College Sports,* edited by Micah L. Issitt, Grey House Publishing, 2021, pp. 25-27.

APA: Joyce, T. (2021). In college sports, non-athletes suffer just as much as the stars on the field. In Micah L. Issitt (Ed.), *The reference shelf: College sports* (pp. 25-27). Amenia, NY: Grey House Publishing.

It's Naïve to Think College Athletes Have Time for School

By Jasmine Harris
The Conversation, October 9, 2018

From my first day as a sociology professor at a university with a Division I football and men's basketball team, education and athletics struck me as being inherently at odds.

Student-athletes filled my courses to take advantage of the fact that the classes met early in the morning.

The football and men's basketball players—most of whom were black—quickly fell behind due to scheduling constraints. Only so much time was set aside for academics and, often, it wasn't enough. Academic rigor and athletic success were simply incompatible goals.

Now—as a researcher who is studying college athletes through the lens of race and class—I have compiled evidence to show just how much more time college athletes devote to sports over academics.

Lopsided but "Normal"

Early data from my ongoing research on the academic experiences of black Division I football and men's basketball players shows that they spend three times as many hours per week on athletics as they do on academics. On average, the players spend more than 25 hours on sports-related activities other than games, such as practice, workouts, general team meetings, film sessions and travel. On the other hand, the players spend less than eight hours on

> **Academic rigor and athletic success were simply incompatible goals.**

academics outside of class, such as writing papers, studying, getting tutored or working on group projects. This imbalance is institutionally constructed and perpetuated. Perhaps most disturbingly, the student-athletes I surveyed perceive this lopsided situation as "normal."

Some may argue that the players should be satisfied with the fact that their scholarships enable them to reap the benefits of a college education. The problem with that argument is that college athletes aren't able to fully actualize their identities as students to the same degree as their classmates. College sports is just too demanding, and universities do not make any special concessions for athletes' additional time commitments.

Money at Stake

It is important to distinguish the lives of college athletes who don't generate money for their institutions, such as soccer and tennis players, versus those who are deeply intertwined with the generation of revenue for colleges, universities and the NCAA, which cleared US$1 billion in revenue in 2017. That kind of money cannot be made without serious time commitments among the players.

Every time I watch a college football or men's basketball game on TV, I can't help but wonder what the players on my screen missed in class that day.

They are students such as Jalen (a pseudonym), a football player who requested a meeting with me mid-semester. He wanted to discuss how my office hours conflicted with the team practices and film sessions. For an hour we discussed what he understood as unfixable. Jalen wanted and needed to utilize the main academic support systems provided by the college, but literally didn't have the time.

Jalen was by no means alone. Rather, his plight was emblematic of untold numbers of college athletes who struggle to balance sports and academics.

Workers or Students?

So, are college athletes workers who attend school part-time? Or are they students who play sports part-time? Players at schools across the country are speaking up about the fact that they generate revenue for the colleges they play for but not for themselves. They have attempted to unionize and filed lawsuits to get what they see as their fair share.

Meanwhile, the NCAA claims that student-athlete balance is not only possible, but that most Division I players achieve it.

Disparities Persist

The reality is most football and men's basketball players underperform academically and routinely graduate at lower rates than "other student-athletes, black non-athletes and undergraduates in general."

Recent academic scandals—from fraudulent classes to inappropriate tutor support and administrative cover-ups—reveal that a sports-first mentality permeates college campuses.

The NCAA continues to describe Division I football and basketball players as "regular students who happen to play sports." However, the NCAA rarely details how this student-athlete balance is supposed to work. There are tournament time commercials that remind viewers how most college athletes "will go pro in something other than sports." However, less mentioned, if at all, are what kind of practical routes exist to this theoretically "balanced" identity. Even the NCAA's own surveys of college athletes show that athletics takes precedence over academics.

Coaches and college staffers are getting rich in the name of higher education while their mostly black players are—in their own words— "broke." And this despite the fact that student-athlete responsibilities have grown as the business of college sports grows. For instance, some of the games last longer, and the average hours that players spend per week on athletes continues to creep upward.

Conflicts Continue

Recently, 2017 Heisman runner-up, Bryce Love, drew criticism for "setting a bad precedent" for choosing to attend summer classes instead of Stanford's media day.

Almost 60 percent of participants in my current national research study find it difficult or very difficult to balance sports and academics—from the moment they set foot on campus until graduation, if they graduate at all. Considering the fact that less than 2 percent of college football players get into the National Football League, and only 1.2 percent of college basketball players get drafted into the National Basketball Association, the reality is that many college athletes will never see a payoff in professional sports. But the real tragedy is that—having devoted so much time to sports instead of their studies—they won't really get to see their college education pay off, either.

Print Citations

CMS: Harris, Jasmine, "It's Naïve to Think College Athletes Have Time for School." In *The Reference Shelf: College Sports,* edited by Micah L. Issitt, 28-30. Amenia, NY: Grey House Publishing, 2021.

MLA: Harris, Jasmine, "It's Naïve to Think College Athletes Have Time for School." *The Reference Shelf: College Sports,* edited by Micah L. Issitt, Grey House Publishing, 2021, pp. 28-30.

APA: Harris, J. (2021). It's naïve to think college athletes have time for school. In Micah L. Issitt (Ed.), *The reference shelf: College sports* (pp. 28-30). Amenia, NY: Grey House Publishing.

Study: College Athletes Have Better Academic, Life Outcomes

By Greta Anderson
Inside Higher Ed, June 24, 2020

College students who participated in athletics tended to fare better than nonathletes in their academic, personal and professional life during college and after graduation, a new Gallup study on alumni outcomes found.

In nearly all aspects of well-being, defined by Gallup as purpose, social, community and physical well-being, former athletes who competed in the National Collegiate Athletic Association were more likely to report they are "thriving" when it comes to health, relationships, community engagement and job satisfaction, according to the report released today. But in one category, financial well-being, former athletes and nonathletes who graduated in the last two decades reported similar levels of student loan debt, with about 20 percent of these graduates exceeding $40,000 in debt, the study found.

The study is part of Gallup's ongoing series examining surveys of college graduates. The study split the 75,000 survey respondents into two different cohorts based on their graduation year, analyzing alumni of 1,900 different colleges and universities in the United States who graduated from 1975 to 1989 and 1990 to 2019, said Jessica Harlan, senior research consultant at Gallup, who authored the report. Some questions also examined how white former athletes and nonathletes compared to their Black peers and the impact athletics had on the success of first-generation college students.

Harlan said the differences between former athlete and nonathlete outcomes are evidence of the "built-in support system" athletics provides throughout a student's college experience, such as mentorship from peers and coaches and direct access to financial aid advisers and academic support. University leaders should find ways to replicate this structure throughout their institutions, she said.

"We know that having a sense of belonging with your peers, having a connection with the university ... these are helpful and promotive for minority students, first-generation students and other underrepresented groups in academia," Harlan said. "These are the things we find that are helping students do well in the athletic programs. How can we bring that to scale for the rest of the student body?"

Amy Perko, chief executive officer of the Knight Commission on Intercollegiate Athletics, said the results of the study exemplify the primary "reasons why college sports should be pre-served and strengthened as part of the educational mission." Student engagement and mentorship, specifically from coaches,

Student engagement and mentorship, specifically from coaches, should be key goals of intercollegiate athletics.

should be key goals of intercollegiate athletics, she said.

But the study also found room for improvement, including in the portion of former athletes, 27 percent, who said they "strongly agree" they had a mentor who "encouraged them to pursue their goals and dreams" during college, Perko said. These results indicate the need for athletics coaches to be better educators, a goal supported by the Knight Commission, which promotes the educational mission of college sports, she said. The NCAA and various coaches' associations have endorsed implementing more development programs for coaches, which Perko said the commission is "encouraged" by.

"Every coach should understand the importance of being a mentor and what that means for student success," Perko said.

Perko said a "significant and important" result is also the Gallup finding that Black graduates who were athletes in college are 10 percent more likely to attain a master's or doctoral degree than Black nonathletes. This could be the result of the financial support that athletes receive if they choose to compete while working toward an advanced degree and of the "enthusiasm and confidence" that athletes in particular have toward pursuing higher education opportunities, Perko said.

Black former athletes also reported that they had more "supportive experiences" than Black nonathletes while they were undergraduates, the study found. Forty-seven percent of Black college athletes said their undergraduate professors "cared about me as a person," whereas 30 percent of Black nonathletes said the same. Black athletes also reported they experienced more mentorship, encouragement to pursue their goals and had professors who made them "excited about learning," according to the study.

"It's a positive report for the educational benefits for college sports, and it reinforces the point that we've tried to make over the years," Perko said. "There's an important role for college sports in higher education, and that role needs to be placed in the proper perspective as part of the educational mission, not apart from it."

Former athletes are also more likely than nonathletes to have earned their bachelor's degree in less than five years, which could be the result of the "external" motivation that academic eligibility requirements from the NCAA provide for athletes, Harlan said. Graduates who were athletes also reported a lower transfer rate than nonathletes, a metric that's "interconnected" with on-time graduation, she said.

"The overarching takeaway is the importance of these supportive experiences from faculty, but also the system that students have to go through, the academic support structure," Harlan said. "We know in general that's critical. NCAA athletics programs on campuses may be one model that universities can look to for how those interact with each other."

Print Citations

CMS: Anderson, Greta. "Study: College Athletes Have Better Academic, Life Outcomes." In *The Reference Shelf: College Sports,* edited by Micah L. Issitt, 31-33. Amenia, NY: Grey House Publishing, 2021.

MLA: Anderson, Greta. "Study: College Athletes Have Better Academic, Life Outcomes." *The Reference Shelf: College Sports,* edited by Micah L. Issitt, Grey House Publishing, 2021, pp. 31-33.

APA: Anderson, G. (2021). Study: College athletes have better academic, life outcomes. In Micah L. Issitt (Ed.), *The reference shelf: College sports* (pp. 31-33). Amenia, NY: Grey House Publishing.

2
The Cost of College Athletics

College track and field and golf teams are often targeted to be cut for budgetary reasons.

The Hidden Perks and Expenses of Collegiate Sports

While collegiate sports bring in tremendous amounts of revenue to colleges and universities, educational institutions also spend heavily to build and maintain their athletics programs. What's more, the effort to continually improve college athletics, and to remain competitive in the field, has led to an increase in the cost of education. The high cost of lucrative and popular sports has also led many educational institutions to streamline their academic offerings, eliminating or reducing funding for other sports and extracurricular student activities.

Deficit Spending

In 2020, the University of Texas recorded more than $220,000,000 in revenues from the school's collegiate athletics programs. The university was one of dozens of universities and colleges that bring in more than 100,000,000 in sports program revenues each year.[1] However, not all schools earn revenues through their sports programs and, for some, funding college sports is a substantial cost. An NCAA study on the finances of intercollegiate athletics found that fewer than 25 percent of schools record a positive net balance from their sports programs. This report also showed that the median loss for schools not earning profit was around $15 million.[2] Across the field, then, while a few fortunate universities can earn millions, for many colleges investing in sports is a significant drain on resources.

If college sports is a losing proposition for so many institutions, then why do universities and colleges continue to invest? The answer lies in the myriad advantages that athletics programs bring to educational institutions. Some universities can draw millions in revenues from media partnerships, ticket sales, donations. But even unprofitable athletics departments have advantages. For one thing, collegiate sports franchises are part of what gives a university or college its identity. Many Americans learn about schools through collegiate teams and performances. Sports teams provide opportunities for branding and marketing, and this draws indirect revenue, especially for those with well-known sports franchises.

The benefits of collegiate athletics are also lasting and multifaceted. Schools with sports franchises enjoy an advantage in alumni and public engagement, as members of the community take pride in the accomplishments of local sports franchises. Alumni and public engagement is a step toward earning donations, grants, and other support from individuals invested in educational institutions in part because pf sports franchise. For alumni especially, following the teams representing one's former educational institution is a way to remain connected with the institution, and this increased can manifest in advantages for the institution. The indirect profits accrued by universities and colleges with athletics programs, especially those with nationally or internationally famous franchises, are such that universities and colleges continue to invest even when the cost of college athletics significantly outweighs the direct financial gains. Yet, critics argue that the college athletics industry is poorly managed and that the entire industry has grown increasingly wasteful at a significant cost to students and their families.

With millions in potential revenue from college sports, why are so many institutions running at a deficit? Part of the answer is that universities and colleges hoping to compete in high-profile intercollegiate contests are engaged in a race to attract high-profile athletes and also audiences as well as to keep their alumni and other donors engaged. In addition to funding scholarships and other programs to attract new athletes, universities and colleges spend money on equipment, sports facilities, and amenities. One of the most significant contributors to inflated athletics budgets is the high cost of hiring top-level coaches. A 2020 USA Today report stated that the average salary for a college football coach was $2.7 million, with top schools sometimes paying tens of millions to coaches and staff to manage their programs.[3]

What's more, the cost of collegiate athletics is increasing. A 2017 report from USA Today noted that investment in college athletes had been increasing markedly over the past decade and found that there was a positive correlation between spending on athletes and athletic performance. Of course, universities and colleges vary widely in terms of initial resources, and big-money institutions enjoy a serious advantage when it comes to building and maintaining competitive franchises.[4] The increasing cost of attracting athletes and other talent to collegiate programs also means that fewer and fewer institutions may be able to afford to offer robust athletics programs or compete in high-profile intercollegiate competitions.

Sources of Revenue

To attract top talent and interest, universities must be willing to spend lavishly. One of the chief criticisms of college athletics is that ultimately citizens pay much of the price for collegiate athletics programs. Many students and their families are unaware that much of what colleges and universities spend to maintain athletics programs comes from nonathlete students in the form of mandatory fees.[5] The amount charged to nonathlete students for athletics programs has also been increasing, and some critics argue that it is unethical to charge students increasing prices for education when the funding is not used to improve educational offerings or to provide any benefits for nonathlete students. In an era where many Americans struggle to afford the increasing cost of higher education or are forced to sacrifice considerably to pay off education loans, many critics feel that it is immoral for universities to increase the cost, and the long-term burden, only to fund programs that offer little to those who pay for them.

However, though some feel collegiate athletics draws too much away from an institution's educational commitments, revenues from collegiate athletics programs can and do allow educational institutions to provide resources that would not otherwise be available. Economic analyses indicate that some colleges and universities use money brought in by high-revenue sports like football and basketball to fund athletic programs for other students. Sports like rowing, fencing, and track and field are often supported through donations and student fees. Revenues from high-dollar sports may therefore subsidize opportunities for students interested in sports that do not bring in significant revenue.

Many popular sports fall into this category, such as swimming, gymnastics, track and field, and even chess. While not all students take an interest in athletics, participating in athletic teams or programs provides enjoyment, exercise, and many educational opportunities. Lessons learned through competitive athletics and the physical advantages of athletic training can have positive benefits for students of any background. When revenues decline and colleges and universities are forced to reduce spending on their athletics programs, many of these prominent but less popular sports are the first to be cut, and this reduces opportunities for many students to explore the challenges and benefits of collegiate sport.[6]

The controversy surrounding spending has intensified since the onset of the COVID-19 pandemic. As colleges and universities struggle to maintain operations with lowered attendance and cope with the risk of disease transmission, many institutions cut funding to athletics programs. Some critics accused universities and colleges of unfairly cutting nonprofit sports instead of profit-driven sports program, and this led to a resurgence in the debate over collegiate sports spending on a broader level. Some sports analysts have argued that the pandemic might provide impetus for universities, colleges, and Americans as a whole to reconsider the culture of college athletics and its increasing cost to students and, ultimately, to American taxpayers as well.

Works Used

Berkowitz, S., and C. Schnaars. "Colleges Are Spending More on Their Athletes Because They Can." *USA Today*. Jul 6, 2017. https://www.usatoday.com/story/sports/college/2017/07/06/colleges-spending-more-their-athletes-because-they-can/449433001/. Accessed 15, May 2021.

Berkowitz, S., and T. Schad. "5 Surprising Findings from College Football Coaches Salaries Report." *USA Today*. Oct 14, 2020. https://www.usatoday.com/story/sports/ncaaf/2020/10/14/college-football-coaches-salaries-five-surprising-findings-data/5900066002/. Accessed 15 May 2021.

"Finances of Intercollegiate Athletics Database." *NCAA*. 2019. https://www.ncaa.org/about/resources/research/finances-intercollegiate-athletics-database. Accessed 15 May 2021.

Hobson, Will, and Steven Rich. "Playing in the Red." *The Washington Post*. Nov 23, 2015. https://www.washingtonpost.com/sf/sports/wp/2015/11/23/running-up-the-bills/?itid=sf_. Accessed 15 May 2021.

Hu, Cynthia. "Non-Revenue Sports Should Not be Scapegoats for Budget Cuts." *The Johns Hopkins News-Letter,* Oct 22, 2020.

"NCAA Finances." *USA Today*. 2019. https://sports.usatoday.com/ncaa/finances/. Accessed 15 May 2021.

Notes

1. "NCAA Finances," *USA Today*.
2. "Finances of Intercollegiate Athletics Database," *NCAA*.
3. Berkowitz and Schad, "5 Surprising Findings from College Football Coaches Salaries Report."
4. Berkowitz and Schnaars, "Colleges Are Spending More on Their Athletes Because They Can."
5. Hobson and Rich, "Playing in the Red."
6. Hu, "Non-Revenue Sports Should Not be Scapegoats for Budget Cuts."

The High but Hidden Cost of College Sports

By Jody Lipford and Jerry Slice

James G. Martin Center for Academic Renewal, December 24, 2015

A barrage of articles in the popular press points out the escalating cost of higher education, rising student debt levels, and the financial struggles many colleges and universities face. Although many factors are at play, we maintain that expenditures of college athletics are a significant factor that are often overlooked, in particular for small schools, especially those with big-time athletic programs.

A recent piece in *USA Today* points out that only 24 of 230 Division I public schools generated sufficient revenues to cover the total costs of their athletic programs, and that each of these schools was a member of one of the "Power Five" conferences (the Atlantic Coast Conference, the Big Ten, the Big Twelve, the Pacific Twelve, and the Southeastern Conference). A more recent piece in the *Chronicle of Higher Education* says that only six of 201 Division I schools cover total athletic costs.

As the Center for College Affordability and Productivity points out, "(w)hen an athletic program cannot cover its expenses through generated revenue, it is forced to rely on allocated funds from the wider institutional budget." These subsidies from the wider institutional budget can be huge, approaching 90 percent of total athletic costs for small schools.

As economists, we wondered, "How much are the costs of college athletics?" In particular, "How much are the costs *per student?*" And of great import, "How do these costs vary with the size of the school and scale of the athletic program?" We estimated these costs using data collected by the federal government under the Equity in Athletics Disclosure Act.

Our investigation reached two important conclusions: The number of students and the scale of the athletic program matter a lot.

Many costs of college athletic programs are largely fixed, varying greatly with the scale of the school's athletic program, but not with undergraduate enrollment. The National Collegiate Athletic Association (NCAA) mandates the numbers of sports, scholarships, and personnel by the athletic program a college or university adopts. Division I-A (or Football Bowl Subdivision) athletic programs are the most expensive, followed by Division I-AA (or Football Championship Subdivision) programs. Division II programs are significantly less expensive, particularly if they don't play football.

In our analysis, we considered schools in each of these categories and also distinguished whether the school was public or private.

Our analysis confirmed our expectations. Because the costs of college athletic programs are largely fixed, costs per undergraduate student are high for small schools and then drop rapidly as the number of students expands, until reaching relatively small values for large schools. Regardless of the number of students, as the level of play moves up, so do the costs.

A few examples help to illustrate the point. Public schools playing at the Division II level without a football program have the lowest costs. (All costs are measured in 2013 dollars.) With 1,000 students, their per-student costs for athletics are about $2,500. If they have more than 3,000 students, their per-student costs fall to around $1,000.

> **Alumni pressure and politics will prevent downsizing of their athletics programs despite the fact that they must be subsidized.**

For public schools playing FBS football, the costs are much higher, but so too are the numbers of students. At 10,000 students the per-student costs are around $4,400; at 20,000 students the costs are about $2,600; and for a truly large state school with 40,000 students, the costs fall to just over $1,500.

These large schools are also the most likely to generate substantial athletic revenues through ticket sales, television contracts, and appearances in the NCAA basketball tournament or a major bowl game. They also benefit from conference revenue sharing.

Because those revenue sources are unlikely, if not impossible for small schools, controlling athletic costs is critical to keeping pressure off the wider institutional budget. If they don't, the subsidy from the institutional budget can become extreme.

Consider a small, private school like our institution, Presbyterian College, with around 1,000 students. Because Presbyterian College aspired to big-time athletics, it made the transition to Division I-AA (FCS) in the late 2000s and today faces athletic costs of about $12,000 per student. Had the college remained a Division II program, costs would be around $5,000 per student.

What about North Carolina Schools?

Flagship state universities, the University of North Carolina at Chapel Hill and North Carolina State University, spend heavily on athletics, but also have large numbers of students. Their per-student costs are about $4,500 and $3,000, respectively. In the analysis by the *Chronicle of Higher Education*, UNC receives subsidies of 11.1 percent of total athletic costs, while NCSU receives slightly less (9.7 percent).

For DI-A (FBS) private schools Duke and Wake Forest Universities, with about 6,500 and nearly 4,800 students, respectively, per-student costs are around $12,000. Western Carolina University, playing at the DI-AA (FCS) level with about 7,000 students, has per-student expenditures of about $1,500, quite low for a school its size. But, according to the *Chronicle*, more than 68 percent of this is subsidized by the institutional budget.

Most of the small North Carolina colleges show reasonably good judgment regarding athletics. Lenoir-Rhyne and Mars Hill Universities, each with around 1,300 students, play at the Division II level, although they could cut costs significantly if they dropped intercollegiate football. Brevard College, at about 700 students, stood out as hopelessly undersized for a Division II school with football, but it recently initiated the sensible move to Division III, where schools offer no athletic scholarships.

If students and parents want to pay for intercollegiate athletics, that is their decision.

The problem is that when they pay the bills to their colleges and universities, little is itemized. Therefore, they don't have a good idea as to the dollars that are going to fund athletics.

They might reasonably think that the board charge goes to pay the external vendor who provides meals at the dining hall, that the room charge is used to amortize the costs of dorms and fund their upkeep, and that lab fees are used to purchase requisite equipment for science classes. But, on the whole, charges are "nontransparent." They're vague, indirect, or hidden.

If students and their parents knew how much they were spending for sports, would they stand for it? Many probably wouldn't.

Suppose that the per-student athletic cost at a small college with Division II football comes to $2,500—and that the school made it clear that students must pay that amount separately, whether they participate in sports or not, or attend any games. Would students and their parents choose to spend $10,000 (over four years) for sports? Or might they prefer to trim $10,000 from their college debt?

What about a school with crumbling infrastructure? $2,500 per student could go a long way towards fixing that problem. Or the funds might be used to hire more full-time faculty and rely on fewer adjuncts.

Money has alternative uses, and we predict that budgetary pressures on small schools, especially those playing at the DI-AA (FCS) level, will intensify, forcing these schools to "right size" their athletic programs. Some will drop to Division II or perhaps even to Division III.

Some schools may drop their football programs entirely. Many will find that they can best compete for value-conscious students by greatly reducing their athletics budget.

Large universities, such as UNC and NCSU, are able to generate sufficient revenues to cover or nearly cover the costs of their athletic programs and continue to play at the Division I level. Alumni pressure and politics will prevent downsizing of their athletics programs despite the fact that they must be subsidized.

There will also be resistance to cutting athletics at small schools. Athletics directors, influential alumni and donors, and many presidents will fight against any downsizing. For now, they have nontransparent pricing to hide behind, but in time, budgetary pressures and competition will force many schools to do so.

Print Citations

CMS: Lipford, Jody, and Jerry Slice. "The High but Hidden Cost of College Sports." In *The Reference Shelf: College Sports,* edited by Micah L. Issitt, 41-44. Amenia, NY: Grey House Publishing, 2021.

MLA: Lipford, Jody, and Jerry Slice. "The High but Hidden Cost of College Sports." *The Reference Shelf: College Sports,* edited by Micah L. Issitt, Grey House Publishing, 2021, pp. 41-44.

APA: Lipford, J., & Slice, J. (2021). The high but hidden cost of college sports. In Micah L. Issitt (Ed.), *The reference shelf: College sports* (pp. 41-44). Amenia, NY: Grey House Publishing.

Pandemic Hits College Sports

By Greta Anderson
Inside Higher Ed, April 24, 2020

Ali Wahab learned on a Zoom call that he would no longer be a wrestler for Old Dominion University.

None of the 32 students in the program would be, either, his coaches said during the hastily arranged virtual meeting earlier this month when they announced the bad news. The university is eliminating the wrestling program, and the decision was made in part because of the coronavirus pandemic.

"Regardless of understanding the circumstances or not, we thought that we were untouchable to getting cut because we're some of the most consistent with our winning," said Wahab, a senior who would have competed in his final year during the 2020-21 academic year. "I'm feeling angry about how they decided to cut wrestling and trying to hold myself back from saying something I shouldn't every time someone talks about it."

He said a "wound is still open" from the cut, which in the end will save the university around $1 million in expenses, a statement published by the university's athletic department said. Current and incoming wrestlers with athletic scholarships such as Wahab will have them for an additional year, which he said is the least the university can do.

Old Dominion wrestling and the University of Cincinnati men's soccer program are the early victims of what are likely to be more sports program cuts as the coronavirus pandemic wreaks havoc on the budgets of universities across the country. More "nonrevenue" athletic programs such as these, which have high operating costs and typically do not bring in any funds for athletic departments, could be on the chopping block as institutions assess the financial damage in the coming weeks and months.

Athletic departments are starting to have tough conversations about where cuts need to be made, said Sam Perelman, a second-year graduate student at Old Dominion and vice chair of the National Collegiate Athletic Association's Student Athlete Advisory Committee, or SAAC. A "very low number" of athletic departments were profitable before the pandemic, and the slowing economy is making it harder for them to keep all their programs, said Perelman, who was speaking personally and not for the SAAC.

"You hate to see it," said Perelman, who played his final year of tennis for Old

Dominion last year. "There is such a financial strain at this point. Not just at ODU, but across the country."

Perelman said most college athletes would hope that all other options are exhausted before programs are cut. But as commissioners of the NCAA's various Division I conferences consider the financial health of their member institutions, they are asking the association to temporarily reduce the number of sports each college is required to sponsor. This puts nonrevenue programs such as volleyball, wrestling, soccer and swimming and diving at risk of "extinction," said Kathy DeBoer, executive director of the American Volleyball Coaches Association.

DeBoer and other leaders in the Intercollegiate Coach Association Coalition, or ICAC, oppose the proposal to waive the sport sponsorship requirement, which they see as a move to allow for the permanent dropping of certain sports, she said. College coaches' associations are discussing ways expenses can be reduced, but DeBoer called the suggestion that institutions should sponsor fewer sports "lethal and cruel and toxic."

"Sports can recover from schedule changes and reductions. Sports can recover from staffing reductions and even scholarship reductions," DeBoer said. "We can recover from anything but extinction. You don't recover from extinction."

Craig Thompson, commissioner for the Mountain West Conference, which is part of the Group of Five, "has been clear it's not about cutting sports," Javan Hedlund, a spokesperson for the conference, said in an email. Hedlund noted that Thompson has repeatedly emphasized that he favors reductions in travel and the number of competitions held rather than elimination of programs. Thompson was not available for an interview.

The 130 institutions in Division I that are part of the Football Bowl Subdivision, or FBS, in which the top football teams in the country compete, are required to sponsor at least 16 athletics programs including football, according to the NCAA's bylaws. A minimum of six of these teams must be men's or mixed gender, and at least eight must be all-female programs, the bylaws say. There are a number of other requirements for institutions to be part of the FBS, such as minimums for financial aid awards granted to athletes and the number of contests scheduled.

All these requirements come at a cost to institutions, and commissioners of the Group of Five conferences, which represent 63 mid-major universities, sent a letter to NCAA president Mark Emmert to ask for a four-year waiver, given the current financial state of higher education. The waiver would provide college officials with "the ability to make prudent and necessary decisions for the financial well-being of the institution" while maintaining the colleges' status as FBS members, said the April 9 letter to Emmert signed by the five commissioners. Commissioners for the remaining 22 Division I conferences, outside the Power Five, have joined this request as well, ESPN reported.

"The COVID-19 pandemic and resultant economic turmoil has resulted in the direst financial crisis for higher education since at least the Great Depression," the letter said. "Providing short-term relief from a handful of regulatory requirements will facilitate the opportunity for institutions to retrench and rebuild the financial structures of the institution."

Large decreases in enrollment, state appropriations, philanthropy and endowment value are having a negative impact on colleges' bottom line, the commissioners explained. Division I institutions also saw a $375 million cut to their NCAA revenue distributions as a result of the cancellation of the March Madness men's basketball tournament, and uncertainty surrounds the 2020-21 college football season.

The letter to Emmert also raises questions about institutions' compliance with Title IX, the law prohibiting sex discrimination at federally funded colleges, which requires an "equal opportunity" for both men and women to participate in sports and receive scholar-

> **Instead of asking individual athletic departments to make cuts, NCAA leaders should be discussing options to reduce operation costs broadly.**

ships. No conference or institution is likely to ask for Title IX compliance waivers, and they shouldn't, said Amy Perko, CEO of the Knight Commission on Intercollegiate Athletics. Institutions with football programs would be left with "narrow" choices on which sports to cut, and nonrevenue men's sports would specifically be at risk should NCAA leadership accept the commissioners' request, she said.

DeBoer said it's "shortsighted" to consider eliminating opportunities for college athletes who receive much fewer scholarships because they play non-revenue-generating sports. These athletes pay tuition and fees, she said.

"This is a time when higher education is losing enrollment," DeBoer said. "We all know that athletics is one of the drivers to enrollment in higher education. It drives kids to college that wouldn't normally go to college."

The pandemic is a time of reckoning for Division I athletic departments, which have historically poured revenue into creating powerhouse facilities and programs but failed to save funds and prepare for a "blip in their system," said Nick Schlereth, a recreation and sport management professor at Coastal Carolina University who studies collegiate athletics' cash flow. Departments are incentivized to build winning teams, not reserves, and if they overspend, they are typically covered by other university funds, he said.

"This is all the product of not being great stewards of the budget," Schlereth said. "There's been a lot of overspending. The times have always been good, and we haven't thought about it."

Less than half of athletic directors at institutions with the nation's top Division I football teams have financial reserves for crises like the current pandemic, according to a recent survey of 100 directors conducted by the LEAD1 Association, which represents the 130 athletic directors in the FBS, and Teamworks, an athlete engagement platform. Forty-one percent of institutions in the Power Five conferences, which are made up of more than 50 large public universities, reported they have financial reserves, while just 26 percent of the Group of Five said they have funds saved.

Institutions in the Group of Five conferences rely much more on student fees and financial support from their universities, according to 2018 athletics budget data collected by the Knight Commission. As universities are beginning to announce revenue losses, hiring freezes and drops in enrollment, Group of Five athletics departments may become financially unstable, Schlereth said.

The Power Five, which includes the Atlantic Coast Conference, Big 12, Big Ten, Pac-12 and Southeastern Conference, collects almost all of its revenue from media-rights contracts for sports broadcasting, postseason football appearances, ticket sales and donors, Knight Commission data show. These universities and their highly competitive and profitable football programs are holding on to hope that the 2020-21 season will be played in some form or fashion. If not, $4.1 billion, an average of $78 million per institution, will be at risk, according to a *USA Today* Sports analysis of Power Five financial reports.

Perko said instead of asking individual athletic departments to make cuts, NCAA leaders should be discussing options to reduce operation costs broadly, particularly the nonrevenue sports, which rely largely on lucrative football and sometimes basketball programs. Discussions about restructuring current conferences "may seem like a radical suggestion," but making them more regionally based, for example, could reduce the cost of athletes' travel, Perko said.

"There's already lots of conversations happening even among the conferences that have the most resources about how to offer some sports competitions in this coming year that are different from their traditional structure, to reduce cost, but also taking into account the crisis we're dealing with," Perko said.

The Division I Council, a 40-member legislative body of intercollegiate athletics officials and student athlete representatives, will meet twice at the end of this week to discuss any national solutions before the NCAA Board of Directors meets on April 28. It's the time to "be creative and maybe even wave in new era of college athletics," said Perelman, who sits on the council.

"Every athletic department is a little bit different, but things are going to have to change," Perelman said. "That's the fact of the matter, at least for the short term."

Print Citations

CMS: Anderson, Greta. "Pandemic Hits College Sports." In *The Reference Shelf: College Sports,* edited by Micah L. Issitt, 45-48. Amenia, NY: Grey House Publishing, 2021.

MLA: Anderson, Greta. "Pandemic Hits College Sports." *The Reference Shelf: College Sports,* edited by Micah L. Issitt, Grey House Publishing, 2021, pp. 45-48.

APA: Anderson, G. (2021). Pandemic hits college sports. In Micah L. Issitt (Ed.), *The reference shelf: College sports* (pp. 45-48). Amenia, NY: Grey House Publishing.

College Athletics Win and Lose Big

By Justin Touhey

Pepperdine University Graphic, November 18, 2020

The Pepperdine University athletic department is composed of a few hundred student-athletes who compete in various sports, all with different financial means and expenses.

The maintenance of Pepperdine Athletics costs a few million dollars per year, and each team has different financial resources. It is one of the largest costs Pepperdine undertakes per year.

Pepperdine is a Division I institution that does not have football, so the biggest expense and potential source of revenue is the men's basketball team.

The total operating expenses of the men's basketball team are $973,890, almost $600,000 more than any other athletic team at Pepperdine as of 2019, according to the Equity in Athletics Data Analysis report.

The next most expensive sport is baseball, with its expenses reaching $376,866. The least-expensive sports are Men's and Women's Cross Country and Track, with its totaling operating expenses reaching $51,404.

Pepperdine Athletics' total revenue for all sports is $23,609,320, and Men's and Women's Basketball make up close to one fourth of that revenue.

Recruiting expenses are $398,711, with the men's recruiting at $248,633 and the women's at $150,078.

Pepperdine Athletics remains in compliance with Title IX and NCAA regulations by having the ratio of male and female student-athletes the same as the student population of males and females enrolled at Pepperdine, according to the NCAA. Pepperdine's male student population is 42% and Pepperdine's female student population is 58%, which is the same ratio for student-athletes in athletics.

Women's teams receive $5,095,296 in athletic-related student aid and the men's teams receive $3,671,261. Women's sports at Pepperdine receive more funding because of Title IX, which measures individual athletes participation based on gender instead of the number of male and female teams at Pepperdine.

The NCAA establishes a maximum number of scholarships for each sport. The scholarships vary in number and athletic aid depending on the institution. Programs are either fully funded, partially funded or receive no funding.

"At Pepperdine, men's and women's basketball, women's tennis, and women's volleyball offer full scholarships. The remaining sports offer partial scholarships.

All sports scholarships except men's and women's cross country/track and women's swim and dive are fully funded," wrote the Assistant Director of Athletics Roger Horne in an email.

Inherent Value of Intercollegiate Athletics

The value of a student-athlete not only enhances an institution's ability to bring in revenue, but it can also offer an advantage when applying for jobs.

Employers view college athletes to be goal-oriented, hardworking and self-confident, according to an article from *USA Today*.

Student-athletes are also more likely to graduate from their institution than non-athletes. The NCAA Division I graduation rate was 89% in 2019, which was the highest it has ever been, according to the NCAA.

While the idea of playing the sport an athlete loves and

> **College sports is now a multibillion-dollar business. Every year the NCAA generates around $7.6 billion in revenue.**

receiving an education for a significant discount is appealing, the NCAA structure, from a business perspective, has changed dramatically from when it was founded in 1906.

The NCAA is a non-profit its mission is to equip student-athletes to succeed in every area of life. The evolution of college sports from a small governing body to a corporate entity has been a slow but steady process.

Amateurism and Intercollegiate Athletics as a Business

College sports is now a multibillion-dollar business. Every year, the NCAA generates around $7.6 billion in revenue, according to an article from *The Conversation*.

Broadcast rights and marketing deals have changed the dynamic of college sports, as more institutions can spend more money on athletic aid, facilities, recruits and travel expenses.

The biggest televised college sporting event is the Division I Men's Basketball Tournament, known as March Madness.

March Madness generates $821.4 million in marketing and television rights and $129.4 million in championship ticket sales, according to an article from *Zacks Investing*.

However, football garners more revenue than the next 35 other sports combined at Division I schools. On average, football brings in $31.9 million in revenue per year for the NCAA, while men's basketball—the second-highest grossing sport—comes in second at $8.1 million per year for the NCAA.

65 of the 350 Division 1 schools in the NCAA are responsible for this revenue, which is fewer than 3% of Division I institutions. The 65 schools make this revenue from their men's basketball and football programs.

Schools like the University of Texas generated $182 million in 2016, and the top

20 programs in the NCAA have generated revenues over $100 million per year from 2016 to 2019.

Despite these sums, the term "amateurism" defines student-athletes. While they are responsible for the product on the court or the field, they cannot profit off their talent or social status until they are out of the NCAA system.

Multibillion—dollar corporations like apparel companies and broadcasting companies are stakeholders in the business of the NCAA. What happens in college sports affects their company's operations and potential profit.

Zion Williamson was the number one pick in the 2019 NBA draft, and he played one year of college basketball at Duke. In Duke's game against the University of North Carolina, Williamson blew out his Nike shoe he was wearing. Later that day, Nike's stock dropped, according to an article from *The Conversation*.

Where the Money Goes

Coaches are some of the highest paid officials in institutions, as some are signing multimillion-dollar contracts.

The average institution salary per head coach for men's teams at Pepperdine is $193,035, and for women's teams it is about $115,380, according to the EADA.

Assistant coaches' salaries for men's teams is an average of $142,989, and for women's teams it is $64,426.

Coaches like Dabo Swinney of Clemson have massive salaries. Swinney, the head football coach, makes $9.3 million per year. Nick Saban of Alabama's salary is $8.6 million.

Facilities and recruiting are also big portions of athletic departments' spending, especially as they become more lavish and sophisticated.

In 2014, 48 schools combined for $772 million combined on athletic facilities, an 89% increase from $408 million spent in 2004, adjusted for inflation. Those figures include annual debt payments, capital expenses and maintenance costs, according to an article from the *Chicago Tribune*.

Football and basketball teams have practice facilities, professional-quality locker rooms, players' lounges with high-definition televisions, video game systems and luxury suites to coax more money from boosters.

During the 2018 fiscal year, public schools in the Southeastern Conference averaged more than $1.3 million in football recruiting costs, compared with public schools in the Big 12 ($961,981), ACC ($938,424), Big 10 ($855,437) and Pac-12 ($708,750), according to an article from the *Courier Journal*.

Financial Impact of COVID-19

The expenses and revenue of college sports has continued to climb steadily over the last decade, but COVID-19 has put many institutions in jeopardy of losing millions of dollars in revenue due to canceled sporting events.

The NCAA canceled all winter and spring sports in March. The men's basketball tournament was a few weeks from beginning.

The cancellation of this tournament cost the NCAA $375 million. The NCAA was set to distribute a total of $600 million to over 1,200 schools before the cancellations, but only distributed $225 million, according to an article from *Market Watch*.

Because most institutions do not make a profit, this multimillion-dollar contribution from the NCAA helps many athletic departments operate.

The West Coast Conference—in which Pepperdine competes—was looking forward to having three teams in the men's tournament. The financial benefit for the conference would have been large because every time a team makes the tournament or advances a round, its conference earns a "unit" to be paid out among its members, according to an article from the *LA Times*.

These "units" contribute to the operational budgets and provide an influx of money for the funding to athletic departments in the conference.

With the NCAA Board of Governors voting to move the fall championships to the spring, institutions are starting to suffer financially.

Since April, more than 250 teams in over two dozen sports have been eliminated across collegiate sports, affecting schools like Minnesota, Iowa, Connecticut and Dartmouth, according to an article from the *New York Times*.

In July, Stanford announced it would be cutting 11 varsity sports including men's wrestling, which had just won a national championship the year before. They also announced that 20 coaches would lose their jobs.

Student-athletes affected the most are the ones whose sport does not generate any revenue for the university such as track and field, swimming, wrestling and rowing, according to an article from USA Today.

Small institutions are having a tough time, but they have been able to weather the storm because their budget is significantly smaller than those whose revenue depends on men's basketball and football.

Schools within the Power Five conference—Pac-12, ACC, Big Ten, Big 12 and SEC—risk massive financial loss.

Ohio State, home to one of the country's premier football programs, has over 40,000 students and a 105,000-seat football stadium. While ticket and concession sales are important, the real money comes from its national broadcast agreements. Last year, the school brought in more than $45 million in revenue for its athletic programs, according to an article from *MarketPlace*.

With the financial impact being so significant, institutions are desperate to forge ahead and have some type of fall sports season.

Three of the Power 5 conferences—the Big 12, ACC and SEC—are having a fall season. The Big Ten and Pac-12 originally postponed but are making a schedule for fall competition to return by Thanksgiving, according to an article by *CBS Sports*.

Positive COVID-19 tests are occurring in institutions all around the country. On Oct. 15, the No. 10 ranked Florida Gators put their football activities on hold after the school announced that the team had five new cases. They were scheduled to play LSU the weekend of Oct. 17, according to an article from *ESPN*.

Conferences also plan to allow fans to come into the stadium in some capacity throughout the season. Most schools will allow the stadiums to be filled between 20 and 25% of normal capacity with COVID-19 guidelines and social distancing in place, according to an article from *Sports Travel Magazine*.

The financial impact of COVID-19 on Pepperdine Athletics, other than the loss of NCAA money from March Madness, is not immediately known.

Print Citations

CMS: Touhey, Justin. "College Athletics Win and Lose Big." In *The Reference Shelf: College Sports,* edited by Micah L. Issitt, 49-53. Amenia, NY: Grey House Publishing, 2021.

MLA: Touhey, Justin. "College Athletics Win and Lose Big." *The Reference Shelf: College Sports,* edited by Micah L. Issitt, Grey House Publishing, 2021, pp. 49-53.

APA: Touhey, J. (2021). College athletics win and lose big. In Micah L. Issitt (Ed.), *The reference shelf: College sports* (pp. 49-53). Amenia, NY: Grey House Publishing.

Colleges Are Eliminating Sports Teams—and Runners and Golfers Are Paying More of a Price Than Football or Basketball Players

By Molly Ott and Janet Lawrence
The Conversation, March 3, 2021

North Carolina Central University, a historically Black college, announced in February that its men's baseball team—which formed in 1911—would cease to exist after this season. The school's athletic director called it "one of the most disappointing days in my career." University leaders concluded that financial shortfalls due to COVID-19 were too much to support the team going forward.

Since COVID-19 emerged, dozens of colleges and universities have announced the elimination of different intercollegiate athletics teams. The vast majority of these cuts are at schools and teams that never show up on *ESPN's SportsCenter*.

As professors who study higher education, we took a closer look at the 300 teams that were dropped between March and October 2020 by 78 colleges and universities.

It's a diverse group of institutions. Some—like Stanford and Brown—have multi-billion-dollar endowments. They compete in the NCAA's Division I, which is the top level of college sports.

But the majority of closures came at regional and local campuses that participate in the NCAA's Division II and Division III, or the National Association of Intercollegiate Athletics. Also, around 30 teams were eliminated by community colleges.

Regardless of campus differences, COVID-19's financial consequences are a shared rationale cited by university leaders for the recent closures. The 78 schools we examined spend around $87 million a year to keep all those teams going.

> **Approximately 500,000 athletes compete across the three NCAA divisions each year.**

The impact of shutting down college sports teams goes beyond an athletic department's bottom line. Many in the sports world have focused on what it means for U.S. participation in the Olympics.

But there are other implications–positive as well as negative–for campuses themselves and how schools attract prospective students.

Entertainment and Cultural Value

Last season was also the final one for the University of Alaska-Anchorage's men's hockey and women's gymnastics programs. In September, UAA's Board of Regents voted to shut down both teams as well as alpine skiing. A last-minute fundraising drive raised over US$600,000 to save the latter.

Most university administrators don't expect their athletics programs to make a lot of money. Only about 25 of the 1,100 NCAA member schools' athletics departments generate a profit. Institutions often spend far more money than their teams will earn from ticket sales, broadcasting contracts and the like. Higher ed leaders say sports provide entertainment and cultural value for students and the local community. Along with civic and performing arts activities, they liven up a campus.

Funding and Donors

Certain sports, like football, are also useful for cultivating donor and political relationships. A 2003 study found that public universities with NCAA Division I football teams received about 6% more in state funding annually than other institutions. And when those football teams win–especially against in-state rivals–state financial support goes up even more the next year.

Research also shows that having a varsity football program increases a school's national visibility and status. Given this, we weren't surprised that only four of the 300 teams eliminated between March and October were football.

A Changing Student Body

Many colleges and universities depend on varsity sports–like rowing, track and swimming–to attract more students to attend. Athletes make up a sizable proportion of the general undergraduate population, especially at smaller schools. For example, NCAA Division III campuses enroll an average of 2,600 students, and one out of every four is a varsity athlete.

Approximately 500,000 athletes compete across the three NCAA divisions each year. Research shows sports is the top factor in athletes' college choice decision– outweighing academics, the campus social scene or proximity to home.

For the 300 teams in our analysis that were recently cut, 2018-19 federal data for each intercollegiate program indicates more than 5,400 athletes were members of those teams each year.

Most students who play college sports–including all of those at Division III and Ivy League programs–are not on an athletic scholarship.

So with fewer sports, the student body at some of these schools might change. For example, Stanford's admissions office will no longer need to reserve 240 or so spots for accomplished fencers, field hockey and squash players, rowers, sailors, synchronized swimmers, men's volleyball athletes and wrestlers.

Cutting those sports could open up new opportunities for applicants with different backgrounds, interests and achievements.

For students themselves, participating in varsity athletics is generally advantageous. Research shows that athletic talent improves an applicant's chances of admission to top schools.

Playing sports can also help with the transition into college. An intercollegiate team provides a ready-made social group that can help the new team member adjust to their new school.

While the demands of big-time programs in men's basketball and football can cause academic challenges for these students, studies have found that overall, athletes perform just as well in classes and have a higher likelihood of graduating compared to other students.

Research also shows that hiring managers value college sports experience. Some studies have found that former athletes have higher salaries and career success, on average, than other post-secondary graduates.

The full implications of the abrupt, unprecedented stop of intercollegiate athletics—and what it means for athletes, coaches, schools and beyond—is still unclear.

Eventually, "big-time" programs like Duke men's basketball and Louisiana State University football will be back to business as usual. For many other schools, COVID-19's effects will be more expansive and long-lasting.

The financial savings for athletics departments are immediate and obvious. But a longer-term impact will be seen on enrollment, campus life and the communities where colleges are located.

Being a team member in a sport that doesn't draw thousands of spectators or bring in millions of dollars still builds special connections to campuses that can foster institutional giving and enhance the health and longevity of participants.

Credit line:

Print Citations

CMS: Ott, Molly, and Janet Lawrence. "Colleges Are Eliminating Sports Teams—and Runners and Golfers Are Paying More of a Price Than Football or Basketball Players." In *The Reference Shelf: College Sports,* edited by Micah L. Issitt, 54-56. Amenia, NY: Grey House Publishing, 2021.

MLA: Ott, Molly, and Janet Lawrence. "Colleges Are Eliminating Sports Teams—and Runners and Golfers Are Paying More of a Price Than Football or Basketball Players." *The Reference Shelf: College Sports,* edited by Micah L. Issitt, Grey House Publishing, 2021, pp. 54-56.

APA: Ott, M., & Lawrence, J. (2021). Colleges are eliminating sports teams—and runners and golfers are paying more of a price than football or basketball players. In Micah L. Issitt (Ed.), *The reference shelf: College sports* (pp. 54-56). Amenia, NY: Grey House Publishing.

Power Five Colleges Spend Football, Basketball Revenue on Money-Losing Sports: Research

By Denise-Marie Ordway
Journalist's Resource, September 10, 2020

Colleges and universities that compete in the nation's five major athletic conferences, known as the Power Five, have collected billions of dollars a year through ticket and merchandise sales, TV contracts and other revenue sources. But less than 7% of it has gone back to the athletes who play the two sports that bring in the bulk of that money—men's basketball and football, a new working paper from the National Bureau of Economic Research finds.

In fact, Power Five institutions, home to the country's wealthiest athletic departments, use most of that revenue to fund less popular sports that tend to lose money and draw students from higher-income families, the analysis shows. Those other sports include women's tennis and men's golf.

It's a business model that, according to the authors, "effectively transfers resources away from students who are more likely to be black and more likely to come from poor neighborhoods towards students who are more likely to be white and come from higher-income neighborhoods."

The authors note that their analysis provides clear evidence that increases in revenue from men's basketball and football lead to increases in spending on other college sports. They also provide estimates for how much schools could pay college athletes if they eventually decide—or are required — to do so.

Author Matt Notowidigdo, an economics professor at the University of Chicago's Booth School of Business, told *Journalist's Resource* that a combination of state legislation and civil litigation is likely to lead to improved compensation for college basketball and football players in the years to come.

"Our paper provides a way to think through some of the economic consequences of this," he wrote via email.

Notowidigdo said the 71-page paper provides new insights across college sports.

"We identify a clear causal relationship between the revenue that is brought in by football and basketball programs and the spending on: other sports (women's sports and other men's sports), absurdly lavish athletic facilities, and exorbitant coaches' salaries," he told *JR*.

Demographics of Power Five College Athletes

Notowidigdo and his colleagues examined data on athletic department revenue and expenses for 64 of the 65 colleges and universities that competed in Power Five conferences between the 2005-2006 academic year and the 2018-19 academic year. They also examined athletic rosters for 2018 to better understand how the demographics of men's basketball and football teams differ from the demographics of students in other sports.

The authors find that about half of men's basketball and football players at Power Five institutions in 2018 were Black, compared with about 11% of athletes in all other sports. Men's basketball and football players also tended to come from lower-income families.

Meanwhile, about 86% of white athletes competed in what the researchers call "non-revenue" sports—those that are not men's basketball and football. Most of those other programs, which include women's sports, consistently operate at a loss, explain the authors, four researchers from the University of Chicago, Northwestern University and the University of Michigan.

"We estimate that the average football and men's basketball athlete went to a high school with a median family income at the 49th percentile of all high schools, while for other sports the average athlete's high school was at the 60th percentile," they write. "In addition, we show that football and men's basketball players come from school districts with a higher fraction of students living in poverty and a higher fraction of students who are black."

Power Five Coach Salaries Soared

The researchers discovered that it's not just students who play non-revenue sports who benefit from the money generated by men's basketball and football. Coaches' salaries across different sports have soared in recent years, Notowidigdo and his colleagues explain.

"In the case of coaches, the economic benefits are startlingly large," they write, adding that football coaches received especially large increases in pay. "In 2018, the average Power 5 conference football coaching staff was paid approximately $9.6 million. This was a marked increase since 2006, when the average staff earned only $4 million."

The authors find that coaches for non-revenue sports at Power Five schools saw their salaries "increase from $7.3 to $12.5 million, which is roughly a 70 percent increase in just a decade."

The researchers also learned that athletes and fans across sports enjoy new and upgraded athletic facilities purchased with funds raised through col-

> College football alone generates more than $4 billion in annual revenue across Power Five schools.

lege football and basketball. This revenue stream, they write, "creates additional athletic opportunities and increases spending available for sports that do not consistently generate enough revenue to cover their costs."

A 2015 analysis from *The Washington Post* showed that over the previous decade, athletic departments in Power Five schools "have built baseball stadiums, volleyball courts, soccer fields, golf practice facilities and ice hockey arenas with money largely derived from powerhouse football teams and, to a lesser degree, men's basketball teams."

College Sports and the Pandemic

The U.S. is the only country that hosts so-called "big-time" sports at colleges and universities, where athletic departments have evolved into complex commercial enterprises. College football alone generates more than $4 billion in annual revenue across Power Five schools, *Fortune* magazine reported last month.

In the wake of the coronavirus pandemic, college administrators have made a lot of changes to their athletic departments. Basketball and football games have been canceled and postponed, meaning there is less money to go around. The authors of this new paper consider those changes further evidence that non-revenue sports rely heavily on money generated by football and basketball.

"Schools such as the University of Akron, Appalachian State University, the University of Cincinnati, and Old Dominion University and many other non-Power 5 schools have eliminated non-revenue sports in response to the economic damage from the pandemic," they write. "In perhaps the largest such move to date, in July 2020 Stanford University announced they would be cutting 11 non-revenue sports."

While many higher education institutions have canceled or postponed games and practices, others have decided to compete in at least some sports. Three of the five conferences that make up the Power Five will compete in football this fall, as will more than 70 Football Bowl Subdivision programs, *FiveThirtyEight* reported on Tuesday.

Student Athletes Do Not Profit

Despite the financial success of football and basketball programs, student athletes are largely prohibited from sharing in the profits. The administrative authority on intercollegiate sports, the National Collegiate Athletic Association, prohibits colleges and universities from compensating athletes aside from providing funding for education-related expenses.

Many colleges offer their student athletes' scholarships and stipends to pay for such things as tuition, housing, meal plans and books. But men's basketball and football players are not the only athletes who receive that financial aid. Students who play non-revenue sports get scholarships and stipends, too.

"At a minimum, a large fraction of these athletes [of non-revenue sports] receive scholarships that offset some or all of their cost of attending college," the authors write. "In addition, recent events around the 'Varsity Blues' college admissions scandal reveal that athletes for these sports can receive preferential admission to colleges they would otherwise not be academically qualified to attend."

A Proposed Wage Structure

While Notowidigdo and his colleagues do not argue for or against paying student athletes, they did develop a wage structure that allows men's basketball and football players to receive about 50% of the revenue generated by their athletic activities. Professional men's basketball and football players in the U.S. collect a similar revenue share as salary.

According to the authors' estimates, each football player at Power Five institutions would receive an estimated $360,000 per year. Basketball players would receive nearly $500,000 a year.

The paper also outlines a differentiated pay structure that would allow star players to earn more than the others. Under that system, the highest paid college football player—the starting quarterback—would earn $2.4 million. The second-highest paid—the wide receiver—would get $1.3 million.

Starting college basketball players would collect between $800,000 and $1.2 million annually.

"The existing compensation to athletes (scholarships plus stipends) would be subtracted from these totals to arrive at the appropriate cash compensation to players," the authors write. "We argue that these compensation estimates represent a plausible benchmark of what athletes could negotiate if they could engage in collective bargaining."

Print Citations

CMS: Ordway, Denise-Marie. "Power Five Colleges Spend Football, Basketball Revenue on Money-Losing Sports: Research." In *The Reference Shelf: College Sports,* edited by Micah L. Issitt, 57-60. Amenia, NY: Grey House Publishing, 2021.

MLA: Ordway, Denise-Marie. "Power Five Colleges Spend Football, Basketball Revenue on Money-Losing Sports: Research." *The Reference Shelf: College Sports,* edited by Micah L. Issitt, Grey House Publishing, 2021, pp. 57-60.

APA: Ordway, D.-M. (2021). Power five colleges spend football, basketball revenue on money-losing sports: Research. In Micah L. Issitt (Ed.), *The reference shelf: College sports* (pp. 57-60). Amenia, NY: Grey House Publishing.

The NCAA Whiffed on Esports: It's Paying a Price but Can Still Learn a Lesson

By Ellen Zavian

The Washington Post, August 6, 2020

The fate of college football and NCAA athletic events this year appear to be in serious jeopardy due to the coronavirus pandemic. Cancellations would carry significant financial repercussions for schools that would lose revenue from events that regularly generate millions. Already, the cancellation of last year's NCAA tournament saw an expected $375 million evaporate from the organization's coffers. Given that financial picture, the NCAA might be kicking itself these days over a decision that its Board of Governors made a little over a year ago, on April 30, 2019. That was the day the NCAA declined to move esports under its governance umbrella.

Today's landscape, due to the pandemic as well as recent legal developments, looks very different than it did in April 2019. And now, as schools scramble for an alternative to revenue-generating live sports events, it's pretty clear the NCAA's desire to cling to its view of amateurism could cost the institution dearly after it discarded a platform that could have helped mitigate, to a degree, past and potential future financial losses around traditional sports.

When the NCAA board unanimously passed on taking esports under its governance, the decision centered on two main concerns, according to its press release: video games are predominantly played by males (which creates possible Title IX complications) and the violent nature of some games is not in line with the NCAA's image. While these concerns are valid, there was also the fact that the existing financial model of individual sponsorships for talented esports players and streamers conflicted with the NCAA's stance on amateurism. In order to accommodate esports, the NCAA would have had to reconcile its stance prohibiting its athletes from capitalizing on their athletic performances, an issue for which the NCAA was already under siege.

The NCAA's position for decades has been that its student-athletes, as it likes to call them, are amateurs and thus, cannot receive anything of value (in-kind or cash) for their athletic talents (beyond their scholarship, room, board and a small stipend that was introduced in 2015). However, in 2019, California became the first state to pass the Fair Pay to Play Act. This law, which goes into effect in 2023, would permit California based collegiate athletes to make money off of their personal brand by capitalizing on their name, image and license (NIL) rights. As of April, some 30 states were discussing legislation similar to the Fair Pay to Play Act or had already begun the approval process. One of the biggest problems with adding esports to the NCAA stable has thus disappeared, but the organization may have already missed its shot to bring esports into the fold.

When the NCAA backed away from esports the void was filled by many smaller organizations, like the National Association of Collegiate Esports (NACE), American Collegiate Esports League (ACEL) and the Electronic Gaming Federation (EGF), to name a few. Under those banners, esports programs are popping up all over the country at schools ranging from Harrisburg to Ohio State.

"Once the NCAA passed on the opportunity, we knew our organization would continue to grow," said Michael Brooks, Executive Director of NACE, which was created in 2016. To date, NACE has over 170 member schools that have provided more than $16 million in esports scholarships.

One of the school presidents on the review committee for the NCAA Board of Governors was University of Kentucky president Eli Capilouto. After leaving the session in which Intersport, a Chicago-based consulting company, provided the NCAA a report on the role esports could play within the NCAA organization, Capilouto realized that no matter what the NCAA decided, esports

In 2019, California became the first state to pass the Fair Pay to Play Act.

were something his school needed to explore further. According to Heath Price, associate chief information officer for the University of Kentucky, the school saw beyond the competitive element and grasped the bigger picture.

"We came at the esports plan as a campus-wide initiative, beyond the 30-40 elite gamers that would be on our roster of players," Price said. "This was a global initiative to engage the entire campus, approximately 30,000 students, as well as our global community."

The idea was to build participant and audience numbers that would attract partners.

Absent March Madness this year, in April, Kentucky announced a virtual basketball tournament using the game "NBA 2K20" that featured a bracket of future students, current students, alumni and fans of the program. According to Price, the university has been quite successful with this and other ventures, partnering with JMI Sports for the naming rights of UK's new esports facility (along with the UK Federal Credit Union), as well as striking a deal with established esports franchise Gen.G.

Those moves are part of a revenue plan designed to "get us to our five-year goal of a revenue stream exceeding high six figures," Price said, adding. "Perhaps it was better the NCAA did not take esports under its wings right now."

The somewhat ironic part of the NCAA's decision to pass on esports was that its board of governors essentially went against the recommendation of Intersport, the consulting group it hired to explore the issue. Over a two-year period, the consultants accumulated the pros and cons of taking on esports from NCAA member schools and presented its findings to the NCAA board.

Kurt Melcher, the Executive Director of esports for Intersport led the task force that ultimately failed to convince the NCAA to take a chance on the competitive video gaming arena. Melcher believes the reservations of the NCAA stemmed from its "inability to get past the fact that gamers might come to college after earning money, have a personal brand already built in their streaming following, and could easily have a sponsorship deal in place with a vendor [for a mouse, keyboard, or monitor], prior to accepting an NCAA scholarship." Although not discussed openly in the meetings, Melcher believed, "the NCAA's amateurism definition was not something they were ready to change, in order to accommodate the esports athletes."

While the "high six figures" short-term goal of UK pales in comparison to the revenue by top-tier basketball schools around the NCAA tournament, it's still a significant sum that can curb some of the losses caused by the pandemic. The schools will continue to have that ability to add esports, but due to its decision the NCAA is missing out. Brooks believes the inability of the NCAA to shift sponsors to esports will impact them for years.

While the NCAA may not get to enjoy revenue from esports, it can still learn a valuable lesson in how its member institutions and student athletes adapt to the new era of NIL rights. While such a landscape will be new to the NCAA's traditional sports, esports programs have been dealing with that dynamic all the while.

Melcher was hired by Intersport and part of the NCAA working group because he started the first collegiate esports team in 2012 while working at Robert Morris University. Melcher remembers how many of the players he was recruiting from high school had in-kind or cash sponsorship deals.

"I knew if we were going to have a successful program, we would have to honor the existing partnerships the players came to our school with," Melcher said. "If we had a mouse deal with the program, we would exclude that student from the mouse company deal if they had a competing mouse deal and make sure that player was not of any promotions that would cause conflict with his existing deal."

NACE rules permit gamers to license names, images and likenesses to sponsors. Its director, Brooks, does not believe that factor cuts into the revenue of the school. In fact, he believes "it is not just about moving money from one group to another," but rather it's the "future for all college athletes and institutions to grow."

"Whether the esports team is part of the athletic department or the engineering school, we believe esports' success is due to its flexibility, allowing the school to obtain sponsorships while encouraging the gamers to develop their own broadcast channel and licenses," Brooks said. "It is all about helping the athlete build their personal brand, which in turn aids the college in the long run."

Print Citations

CMS: Zavian, Ellen. "The NCAA Whiffed on Esports: It's Paying a Price but Can Still Learn a Lesson." In *The Reference Shelf: College Sports,* edited by Micah L. Issitt, 61-64. Amenia, NY: Grey House Publishing, 2021.

MLA: Zavian, Ellen. "The NCAA Whiffed on Esports: It's Paying a Price but Can Still Learn a Lesson." *The Reference Shelf: College Sports,* edited by Micah L. Issitt, Grey House Publishing, 2021, pp. 61-64.

APA: Zavian, E. (2021). The NCAA whiffed on esports: It's paying a price but can still learn a lesson. In Micah L. Issitt (Ed.), *The reference shelf: College sports* (pp. 61-64). Amenia, NY: Grey House Publishing.

As Partnerships Emerge, Are College Sports Embracing Betting Sponsors?

By Amanda Christovich

Front Office Sports, September 11, 2020

As college sports faces a reckoning on athlete compensation, amateur status and a slew of other issues, yet another long-standing NCAA tradition appears to be falling: the shunning of sports betting operators in the college athletics business.

A partnership between the sports betting operator William Hill and University of Nevada, Las Vegas in 2017 and University of Nevada Reno in 2018, along with the recent partnership launch between PointsBet and the University of Colorado, Boulder, have shown that deals between sports betting companies and collegiate athletic departments can exist despite the NCAA's aversion to sports betting.

While companies and experts remain unsure about how many partnerships between athletic departments and sports betting operators could materialize in the near future, they point to a number of factors that make the landscape ripe for more of these deals: the frequency of sports betting partnerships in professional sports, the growing legality of betting on college sports in the U.S., the new ways of approaching responsible gambling education, and the pandemic-induced economic crisis facing athletic departments.

"I think this one has some momentum," said Michael Goldman, a sports marketing professor at the University of San Francisco, of the potential trend of more of these types of deals.

The stage for sports betting operators to secure partnership deals with U.S. leagues was first set in 2015, when daily fantasy sports advertising blossomed, said Brett Abarbanel, the director of research for the UNLV International Gaming Institute. From there, advertising with individual teams and leagues began as well, and the 2018 U.S. Supreme Court decision to strike down the federal ban on sports gambling opened the door for many individual states to legalize sports betting.

Sports betting operators abroad had already mastered the sponsorship market with professional leagues, said Goldman, and the way to do that in the U.S. is "manage your stakeholders and capture your regulators." That means sports betting operators must "position" themselves to be in the interests of the fans and teams, and use "good-old U.S. lobbying" to break down existing laws that might limit sports betting operations, he said.

In the college space, sports betting operators are beginning to position themselves not only as legal and responsible, but also companies that fans and alumni use.

Deals between sports betting companies and collegiate athletic departments can exist despite the NCAA's aversion to sports betting.

The process hasn't been quick, however, which could explain why the first new partnership since 2018 is only cropping up now, said Abardanel. But now, the landscape is primed for these partnerships to become more common.

Both William Hill and PointsBet serve as examples of companies looking to position themselves as a positive force in their local sports markets, and particularly in college sports.

The 2017 William Hill deal began when a Learfield employee at UNLV reached out to an old friend named Michael Grodsky, who serves as William Hill's vice president for marketing in Nevada. "I've never responded to an email that quickly, saying we'd love to figure it out," said Grodsky about securing a partnership with UNLV.

It was the first time the company had discussed a partnership with a college athletic department, Grodsky said, but certainly not the last—in 2018, the sports betting operator secured a similar partnership with University of Nevada, Reno.

Learfield IMG College brokered the PointsBet deal, while Learfield brokered the William Hill deals prior to its completed merger with IMG College in 2018. In a statement, the college said it worked with athletic departments to consider "those brands and categories that align with the goals and objectives of the universities." Beau Orth, the Learfield employee who worked on the UNLV deal, was not immediately available for comment.

The deals with Nevada schools particularly invigorated William Hill because of the way they were centered around the Nevada community. "That was really exciting for us, because both universities are so vital to our state," Grodsky said. "We take pride in that."

The most important way to gauge the worth of a sponsorship deal on the sponsors' side is to monitor whether the deal rakes in more customers, Goldman noted. While Grodsky didn't specify, he did say that William Hill is very happy with their partnerships. And given that college sports betting has been legal in Nevada for a while, it isn't surprising that this deal would help William Hill make headway in a crowded sportsbook landscape.

"Because it's getting so competitive, we now want to take advantage of the marketing and communication assets that exist to get in front of our competitors," Goldman said of the need for sports betting operators in the U.S. to develop partnerships.

Print Citations

CMS: Christovich, Amanda. "As Partnerships Emerge, Are College Sports Embracing Betting Sponsors?" In *The Reference Shelf: College Sports,* edited by Micah L. Issitt, 65-67. Amenia, NY: Grey House Publishing, 2021.

MLA: Christovich, Amanda. "As Partnerships Emerge, Are College Sports Embracing Betting Sponsors?" *The Reference Shelf: College Sports,* edited by Micah L. Issitt, Grey House Publishing, 2021, pp. 65-67.

APA: Christovich, A. (2021). As partnerships emerge, are college sports embracing betting sponsors? In Micah L. Issitt (Ed.), *The reference shelf: College sports* (pp. 65-67). Amenia, NY: Grey House Publishing.

3

Lives on the Line

2009 Harvard Crimson and Brown Bears game by chensiyuan, CC BY-SA 4.0, via Wikimedia.

College football is one of the main causes of traumatic brain injury in student athletes.

Health Risks to Student Athletes

While participating in athletics is a great way to build strength and speed, athletes also risk their health by participating in competitive sports. Concussions, back and knee injuries, and other kinds of medical problems are common in athletes of all ages, to the point that many communities are now debating whether certain sports are appropriate for younger athletes. Controversially, colleges and universities often offer little in the way of assistance for injured players, and this is one of the issues often cited by critics and reformers in the field.

How Common Are Sports Injuries?

According to a 2015 study published in the *Morbidity and Mortality Weekly Report* from the CDC, there were 1,053,370 injuries among NCAA athletes for the 2013–2014 season, out of 176.7 million exposures (meaning situations in which an athlete could potentially have been injured). The potential for injury varied widely among different sports. College football players, for instance, were most likely to get injured playing the game, but wrestling had the highest injury rate overall.[1]

Other studies have found similar results, with as many as 20 percent of NCAA athletes experiencing injuries that required a week or more for recovery. In college football, there are more than 20,000 injuries recorded each year, which includes 4,000 knee injuries and 1,000 spinal injuries. While injury rates for other sports are not well known, injuries are also common in wrestling, baseball, hockey, and basketball. Overuse injuries were the most common type of injury recorded for college athletes, and most of these were recoverable and not considered severe. But even seemingly minor injuries can have serious consequences.[2]

Intensity of activity is the key factor in injury statistics. Division I athletes may need to dedicate as much as 30–40 hours per week to exercise and may spend more than 4 hours per day engaged in practice, exercise, or other activity with the potential to cause injury. Added to this are the demands of academic commitment and the nature of college life, meaning that college athletes are less likely to dedicate sufficient time to sleep and recovery and often lack adequate nutrition. This combination puts college athletes at an extremely high risk for certain kinds of injuries, especially those from overuse and muscular injuries.[3]

Concussions and Mobility

By far the most concerning and oft-debated kind of sports injury is concussion, a type of traumatic brain injury (TBI) that occurs when an individual receives a blow to the head or to the body that causes the brain to rapidly shift or twist within the skull. When this occurs, areas of the brain may be damaged and there are chemical changes in the brain that can also cause problems. People with concussions can experience a variety of symptoms, including headaches, difficulty thinking or recalling information, loss of motor control, loss of consciousness, or mood and behavior changes. They may become nauseous, experience problems with balance or vision, or have difficulty adjusting to light or noise. Symptoms can immediately follow an injury or manifest several days later.

While a minor concussion may present little or no danger to an athlete, severe concussions can leave an injured person with lifelong symptoms. Individuals with severe concussions can have long-term problems with cognition and memory, learning, or managing their emotions. On a more physical level, concussion sufferers may have long-lasting problems with speech, hearing, or vision and may have difficulty with coordination and balance.[4]

According to the CDC, 1.6 to 3.8 million sports-related concussions occur in the United States each year. CDC data also indicates that 10 percent of contact sports athletes experience a concussion once per year. Concussion is most common in boxing (where at least 87 percent of professionals have sustained lasting brain injuries) and in football, where data suggests there is at least one concussion for every five football games played. At least 10 percent of college football players and 20 percent of high school players will suffer a brain injury at some point during their time playing the game.[5]

Concussions are one of the most concerning types of sports injuries because many concussions are never diagnosed and, further, damage to the brain is cumulative. Studies indicate that a person who experiences one concussion is up to 6 times more likely to suffer another concussion. Each time an athlete's brain is injured, there is an increased chance that he or she will suffer long-lasting or severe injury; athletes who suffer multiple concussions are at high risk for developing problems later in life, such as chronic traumatic encephalopathy (CTE), a neurogenerative disorder. Repeated studies have shown that boxers and football player are at extremely high risk for developing CTE, which may not appear until much later in life. A 2017 study published in the *Journal of the American Medical Association* found evidence of CTE in 110 of 111 former NFL players studied and in 48 of 53 former college football players.[6]

The public debate over the risk of concussions and complications like CTE tends to focus on professional football players and on high school players, out of a concern for child welfare, but studies indicate that college players are also at extremely high risk. Greg Ploetz, who played football in college but did not enter a professional league, developed CTE in his 60s, which led to severe emotional and cognitive decline, a loss in motor control, and an inability to speak; Ploetz required 24-hour nursing care. While Ploetz's CTE is among the worst diagnosed outside of professional sports, his experience raises serious questions about the welfare of college athletes over the longer term.[7]

Concussion is only one of the many types of injuries frequently suffered by athletes. But the concussion controversy touches on the broader issue of student athletics and injury. Student athletes, to remain competitive, must dedicate significant time and effort to perfecting their sport, increasing their exposure to risk and injuries that can be, in extreme cases, fatal or life changing. Critics argue that American culture must engage in a serious discussion about the value of student athletics in light of the risk to student athletes.

Risks and Rewards

Research indicating that sports injuries are more common and have long-lasting effects has fueled public debates over health and welfare in professional and amateur athletics. Like professional athletes, college athletes are at elevated risk for injuries. Yet, unlike professional athletes, college athletes are not paid for playing and are not guaranteed any medical coverage. While the NCAA requires that student athletes have medical coverage options available to them, the organization does not require colleges or universities to subsidize this coverage or to cover the costs of injuries and recovery. Further, many college athletes receive partial or full scholarships for playing on a sports team, but if they are injured and temporarily or permanently unable to continue performing, colleges and universities are not required to maintain scholarship assistance. An injured college athlete may face personal financial hardship, a loss of educational opportunities, and potentially lasting physical difficulties.[8]

Some critics argue that because NCAA athletes bring in millions in revenue for colleges and universities and indirect revenue for cities and states, colleges and universities should provide medical coverage for those who experience injuries while playing for collegiate sports franchises. While the NCAA offers some programs to help cover the expenses of injuries, such as a Student-Athlete Disability Insurance program, programs like these are helpful only in a small minority of cases because they only cover athletes whose injuries are severe enough that they will never be able to play again. Further, this is an option that student athletes must purchase with their own money. An evaluation of disability insurance by Kevin Fixler published in *The Atlantic* found that the NCAA had only paid out about twelve claims under their disability insurance program in 20 years. In Fixler's assessment, disability insurance is hardly worth the cost for the vast majority of athletes.[9]

While serious injury is always a concern, a far larger number of athletes each year suffer one of the more common types of injuries, like strains, fractures, pulled tendons, and overuse injuries. While these kinds of injuries might not be life-threatening, they can have a lasting effect on an individual's mobility and physical capabilities and still present student athletes with considerable cost. Repairing injured knees, for instance, costs an average of $11,000, though the cost can be substantially higher. This is one of the most common injuries for football players, and the side effects of such an injury can be significant. Players with injuries to their legs, backs, or arms may require years of expensive medical assistance or surgeries, and many suffer long-term impairment. None of these injuries is automatically covered for NCAA athletes, which means that student athletes, especially those without significant resources, not only risk their health and welfare but also their financial wellbeing each time they sign on to play.

While college sports injuries have been a risk for young athletes for many years, 2020 and 2021 brought a new set of COVID-19-related risks. Playing professional sports typically means close contact, which dramatically increases the risk of transmitting airborne illness. As the United States, and the global community, faced the COVID-19 crisis, new questions arose about athletics. Athletes who continued to play also faced increased risk of contracting the disease and then of potentially spreading it to family and loved ones. As with the broader question about injury, the risk of COVID-19 raised questions about the degree to which educational institutions should be responsible for the health and welfare of players. An investigation at Clemson University found that insurance plans offered by the university for athletes would not cover COVID-related illness because the plans only covered injuries resulting directly from competitions or practice. Because athletes might contract COVID-19 outside of their participation in sports, Clemson's student athlete insurance would not provide coverage.[10]

Whether facing COVID-19, concussion, or any other injury, student athletes assume substantial risk. In some cases, they assume this risk on their own with little or no support from universities or the NCAA. Given the considerable revenues and global interest in college sports, and the rewards enjoyed by those who play at this level, there is more than enough incentive to maintain the industry. But can the industry be reformed to protect the athletes who risk their health and welfare to keep the college sports going?

Works Used

Billitz, Jess. "19 College Athlete Injury Statistics (The Risk of Sports)." *Noobgains.* Nov 12, 2020. https://noobgains.com/college-athlete-injury-statistics/. Accessed 18 May 2021.

Fixler, Kevin. "The $5 Million Question: Should College Athletes Buy Disability Insurance?" *The Atlantic.* Apr 11, 2013. https://www.theatlantic.com/entertainment/archive/2013/04/the-5-million-question-should-college-athletes-buy-disability-insurance/274915/. Accessed 20 May 2021.

"Heads Up." *CDC.* 2021. https://www.cdc.gov/headsup/basics/concussion_symptoms.html. Accessed 18 May 2021.

Hruby, Patrick. "The NCAA Is Running Out of Excuses on Brain Injuries." Deadspin. May 24, 2018. https://deadspin.com/the-ncaa-is-running-out-of-excuses-on-brain-injuries-1819854361.

Kerr, Zachary Y., et al. "College Sports-Related Injuries United States, 2009-10 through 2013-14 Academic Years." *Morbidity and Mortality Weekly Report (MMWR).* Dec 11, 2015. https://www.cdc.gov/mmwr/preview/mmwrhtml/mm6448a2.htm. Accessed 16 May 2021.

"Madness, Inc.: How College Sports Can Leave Athletes Broken and Abandoned." *Chris Murphy.* 2019. https://www.murphy.senate.gov/imo/media/doc/Madness%203...pdf. Accessed 17 May 2021.

Mez, Jesse, Daniel H. Daneshvar, and Patrick T. Kiernan. "Clinicopathological Evaluation of Chronic Traumatic Encephalopathy in Players of American

Football." *JAMA*. Jul 25, 2017. https://jamanetwork.com/journals/jama/fullarticle/2645104. Accessed 20 May 2021.

Spector, Jesse. "Will Colleges Cover Medical Bills for Athletes Who Get COVID-19? Don't Count on It." *Deadspin*. Jul 02, 2020. https://deadspin.com/will-colleges-cover-medical-bills-for-athletes-who-get-1844251705. Accessed 20 May 2021.

Walsh, Meghan. "'I Trusted 'Em': When NCAA Schools Abandon Their Injured Athletes." *The Atlantic*. May 1, 2013. https://www.theatlantic.com/entertainment/archive/2013/05/i-trusted-em-when-ncaa-schools-abandon-their-injured-athletes/275407/. Accessed 20 May 2021.

"What Is a Concussion?" *BIRI*. Brain Injury Research Institute. 2021. http://www.protectthebrain.org/Brain-Injury-Research/What-is-a-Concussion-.aspx. Accessed 19 May 2021.

Notes

1. Kerr, et al., "College Sports-Related Injuries–United States, 2009-10 through 2013-14 Academic Years."
2. "Madness, Inc.: How College Sports Can Leave Athletes Broken and Abandoned."
3. Billitz, "19 College Athlete Injury Statistics (The Risk of Sports)."
4. "Heads Up," *CDC*.
5. "What Is a Concussion?" *BIRI*.
6. Mez, Daneshvar, and Kiernan. "Clinocopathological Evaluation of Chronic Traumatic Encephalopathy in Players of American Football."
7. Hruby, "The NCAA Is Running Out of Excuses on Brain Injuries."
8. Walsh, "'I Trusted 'Em': When NCAA Schools Abandon Their Injured Athletes."
9. Fixler, "The $5 Million Question: Should College Athletes Buy Disability Insurance?"
10. Spector, "Will Colleges Cover Medical Bills for Athletes Who Get COVID-19? Don't Count on It."

Murphy Takes on NCAA on College Sports Injuries

By Ana Radelet

The CT Mirror, December 16, 2019

Washington—Sen. Chris Murphy on Monday released his third critical report on college athletics, focusing on what he considers the failure to protect student athletes from devastating and sometimes fatal injuries.

"Across college sports, too many athletes leave their collegiate careers broken," said Murphy's report, "Madness Inc.: How College Sports Can Leave Athletes Broken and Abandoned."

At a press conference in Hartford, Murphy said "I know how important athletics is to the development of a young person."

But he said college athletic programs, especially football programs that earn schools millions of dollars, turn a blind eye to the dangers posed by athletic competition and the rigors of training, "leaving behind athletes who are poor and whose bodies remain broken."

Murphy said he has developed a bipartisan "working group" with other senators, including Mitt Romney, R-Utah, Marco Rubio, R-Fla., Cory Booker, D-N.J., and David Perdue, R-Ga., to determine whether federal legislation is needed to reform college sports.

And a state legislator, Rep. Derek Slap, D-West Hartford, said he is considering state legislation to address problems on the field.

"We can't wait for the NCAA to make the right decisions," Slap said.

At the same press conference, former Notre Dame football player Alan Sack, who played on the school's 1966 national championship team, said some college coaches physically and verbally abuse their players.

"The NCAA is a disgrace," Sack said.

The National Collegiate Athletic Association did not have an immediate response.

But Mark Emmert, president of the NCAA—will meet with Murphy and Romney on Tuesday on Capitol Hill after the initial meeting of the bipartisan working group on campus athletics.

The NCAA has given schools concussion protocols that tell them how to treat players with head injuries, a protocol some neurologists say is not strict enough and not always followed.

In August, the NCAA settled several lawsuits by agreeing to pay $70 million to cover medical testing and diagnosis for former athletes and put $5 million toward concussion and injury research. About 4 million former athletes could be affected by the settlement.

Murphy's study said that nearly 20 percent of college athletic directors reported instances where a coach played an athlete who had been deemed "medically out of participation," putting them at risk for severe injuries.

"That is because coaches are driven to win by the tremendous amount of money in college athletics," Murphy said.

His report detailed some of the best-known tragedies in college sports, including the stories of Kyle Hardrick, a University of Oklahoma basketball player who lost his scholarship and was left with unpaid medical bills after suffering a torn meniscus for which his college didn't want to pay; and

> **40 college athletes have died playing football since 2000 and there are about 20,000 injuries every year in the NCAA.**

Doug Ploetz, a former Texas Longhorn who lost his life to dementia caused by repeated head trauma during his football career.

And then there's the case of Jordan McNair, a University of Maryland football player who died after a punishing training session in sweltering heat," led by coaches who disregarded athlete safety for the sake of toughening up or punishing athletes," the report said.

In all, Murphy's report said, 40 college athletes have died playing football since 2000 and there are about 20,000 injuries every year in the NCAA.

Murphy's latest report on the NCAA is his third. The senator's first report, released in March, examined the billions in revenues produced by college sports and how that money enriches nearly everyone but the athletes themselves because of the NCAA's ban on player compensation.

Murphy's second report examined the ways colleges fail to provide athletes the education they deserve.

"This isn't the most important issue in Connecticut or the nation," Murphy said. "But to me it's an issue of civil rights."

That's because most of the students who are mistreated by the nation's colleges are black and the people who exploit them and profit from their athletic prowess are white, Murphy said.

The senator recommended several reforms.

Those include requiring all college athletes to have heath care coverage, a requirement some schools lack, and that college athletes have access to independent health care providers.

Murphy also recommends that athletes should be able to keep their scholarships if they quit sports and students should be allowed to transfer to other schools.

Murphy's final recommendation could be the toughest to implement.

"There should be real consequences for schools that don't follow health protocols," he said.

As far as legislation to implement some of these reforms?

"Admittedly, this will be a heavy lift," Murphy said.

Print Citations

CMS: Radalet, Ana. "Murphy Takes on NCAA on College Sports Injuries." In *The Reference Shelf: College Sports,* edited by Micah L. Issitt, 77-79. Amenia, NY: Grey House Publishing, 2021.

MLA: Radalet, Ana. "Murphy Takes on NCAA on College Sports Injuries." *The Reference Shelf: College Sports,* edited by Micah L. Issitt, Grey House Publishing, 2021, pp. 77-79.

APA: Radalet, A. (2021). Murphy takes on NCAA on college sports injuries. In Micah L. Issitt (Ed.), *The reference shelf: College sports* (pp. 77-79). Amenia, NY: Grey House Publishing.

College Sports–Related Injuries—United States, 2009–10 through 2013–14 Academic Years

By Zachary Y. Kerr, Stephen W. Marshall, Thomas P. Dompier, et al.
Centers for Disease Control Morbidity and Mortality Weekly,
December 11, 2015

Sports-related injuries can have a substantial impact on the long-term health of student-athletes. The National Collegiate Athletic Association (NCAA) monitors injuries among college student-athletes at member schools. In academic year 2013–14, a total of 1,113 member schools fielded 19,334 teams with 478,869 participating student-athletes in NCAA championship sports (i.e., sports with NCAA championship competition) (1). External researchers and CDC used information reported to the NCAA Injury Surveillance Program (NCAA-ISP) by a sample of championship sports programs to summarize the estimated national cumulative and annual average numbers of injuries during the 5 academic years from 2009–10 through 2013–14. Analyses were restricted to injuries reported among student-athletes in 25 NCAA championship sports. During this period, 1,053,370 injuries were estimated to have occurred during an estimated 176.7 million athlete-exposures to potential injury (i.e., one athlete's participation in one competition or one practice). Injury incidence varied widely by sport. Among all sports, men's football accounted for the largest average annual estimated number of injuries (47,199) and the highest competition injury rate (39.9 per 1,000 athlete-exposures). Men's wrestling experienced the highest overall injury rate (13.1 per 1,000) and practice injury rate (10.2 per 1,000). Among women's sports, gymnastics had the highest overall injury rate (10.4 per 1,000) and practice injury rate (10.0 per 1,000), although soccer had the highest competition injury rate (17.2 per 1,000). More injuries were estimated to have occurred from practice than from competition for all sports, with the exception of men's ice hockey and baseball. However, injuries incurred during competition were somewhat more severe (e.g., requiring ≥7 days to return to full participation) than those acquired during practice. Multiple strategies are employed by NCAA and others to reduce the number of injuries in organized sports. These strategies include committees that recommend rule and policy changes based on surveillance data and education and awareness campaigns that target both athletes and coaches. Continued analysis of surveillance data will help to understand whether these strategies result in changes in the incidence and severity of college sports injuries.

Among all sports, men's football accounted for the largest average annual estimated number of injuries (47,199) and the highest competition injury rate (39.9 per 1,000 athlete exposures).

During the 5 academic years from 2009–10 through 2013–14, injuries and athlete-exposures were voluntarily reported to NCAA-ISP by participating team athletic trainers, using a web-based platform. The number of teams participating in NCAA-ISP varied by sport and year (2). Overall, participation among teams for the study period ranged from a low of 0.7% in men's tennis to a high of 13.2% in men's ice hockey. Data were aggregated across all schools and across all available years for 12 men's championship sports and 13 women's championship sports. Variables examined included the sport, whether the injury occurred during practice or competition, and whether the player required emergency transport, surgery, or ≥7 days before return to full participation. Injuries were defined as those that occurred in an organized NCAA-approved practice or competition and required medical attention by a physician or athletic trainer (2). An athlete-exposure was defined as one student-athlete's participation in one practice or one competition. Injury rates were calculated by dividing the number of injuries by the number of athlete-exposures. Competition-to-practice injury rate ratios were calculated by dividing the competition injury rate by the practice injury rate. To create national estimates, each injury and exposure was assigned a sample weight on the basis of the inverse of the school selection probability, using stratifications based on sport, division, and academic year (3). The national estimates were then adjusted for potential underreporting (3). For example, over the 5-year study period, among the 123 team seasons of men's football from which data were acquired, 8,680 injuries from 899,321 athlete-exposures were reported by participating team athletic trainers. These data, when weighted and adjusted, produced national estimates of 235,993 injuries and 25,770,273 athlete-exposures (or estimated annual averages of 47,199 injuries and 5,154,055 athlete-exposures).

Among all 25 sports, an estimated 28,860,299 practice athlete-exposures and 6,472,952 competition athlete-exposures occurred each year. The 1,053,370 injuries estimated during the 5 academic years studied represented an average of 210,674 total injuries per year, among which, 134,498 (63.8%) occurred during practices. Overall, 21.9% of all injuries required ≥7 days before return to full participation (competition: 24.6%; practice: 20.5%). Among all injuries, those incurred during competition were somewhat more severe than those acquired during practice; overall, 4.0% of injuries required surgery (competition: 5.4%; practice: 3.1%), and 0.9% required emergency transport (competition: 1.4%; practice: 0.6%). These data equated to estimated annual averages of 46,231 injuries that required ≥7 days before the athlete could return to full participation; 8,367 that required surgery; and 1,904 that required emergency transport. Approximately half of all injuries were diagnosed as sprains or strains (competition: 45.9%; practice: 45.0%). Sprains (including anterior cruciate ligament tears) and strains also accounted for the largest proportions of injuries in competition and practice requiring ≥7 days before return to full participation, (52.1% and 47.8%, respectively) and the largest proportion of injuries requiring surgery (57.7% and 52.9%, respectively). In addition, sprains and strains accounted for the largest proportion of practice-related injuries requiring emergency transport (29.4%); however, during competition, the largest proportions of injuries requiring emergency transport were fractures, stress fractures, dislocations, and subluxations (25.8%), and concussions (22.0%).

Among men's sports, football accounted for the largest percentage of athlete-exposures (14.6% of all athlete-exposures and 31.2% of all male athlete-exposures), and football teams were estimated to have the highest number of injuries per year (47,199; 22.4% of all injuries and 36.3% of all male injuries). Football also had the highest competition injury rate (39.9 injuries per 1,000 athlete-exposures) and competition-to-practice rate ratio (6.8) and the third highest overall injury rate (9.2 per 1,000). Overall, football accounted for the largest proportions of injuries requiring ≥7 days before return to full participation (26.2%), surgery (40.2%), and emergency transport (31.9%). Men's wrestling had the highest overall injury rate (13.1 per 1,000 athlete-exposures) and the highest practice injury rate (10.2 per 1,000). Swimming and diving had the lowest overall injury rate (1.7 per 1,000). The rates of injury during competition were higher than during practice for all men's sports. However, more injuries occurred in practices than in competitions for all men's sports except ice hockey and baseball.

Among women's sports, soccer accounted for the highest estimated number of injuries per year (15,113), and the highest competition injury rate (17.2 per 1,000); the competition-to-practice rate ratio was 3.1. Gymnastics had the highest overall injury rate (10.4 per 1,000 athlete-exposures) and practice injury rate (10.0 per 1,000). The lowest overall estimated injury rate (1.8 per 1000) was for swimming and diving. Injury rates were significantly higher during competitions than practices for all women's sports except volleyball, indoor track, and swimming and diving. Compared with practice injuries, a larger proportion of competition injuries required ≥7 days before return to full participation for eight of the 13 women's sports. However, more injuries occurred in practices than in competitions for all women's sports because more than twice as many athlete-exposures each year occurred in practices compared with competition (55,670 versus 25,004).

Among men and women, overall injury rates were similar for soccer, swimming and diving, tennis, and both indoor and outdoor track and field. However, overall injury rates were significantly higher among men than women in basketball, ice hockey, and lacrosse. Overall injury rates were significantly higher among women than men in cross country.

Discussion

Men's football accounts for the most college sport injuries each year, as well as the largest proportions of injuries requiring ≥7 days before return to full participation, or requiring surgery or emergency transport. Thus, prevention efforts that focus on football will target the largest number of severe injuries. The large overall number of football-related injuries is attributable to football having the largest number of student-athletes (71,291 during the 2013–14 academic year) among all 25 reported NCAA sports (16.1%) (2). Although wrestling had the highest overall injury rate among all 25 reported NCAA sports, the number of student-athlete wrestlers was much smaller (6,982). At the same time, the competition injury rates in wrestling and football were nearly equivalent, although the practice injury rate in wrestling was higher than that in football. Among women's sports, gymnastics had the highest rate of injury each year, whereas soccer contributed the largest number of injuries. Many of these data are consistent with earlier reports and can be used to guide resource allocation decisions and research to identify specific risk factors or to evaluate prevention measures (4). It is also important to note that the injury rates reported from these data are higher than those reported from NCAA-ISP before 2004–05 (4) because, unlike previous estimates, rates since the 2009–10 academic year have included injuries requiring <1 day before return to full participation.

The relationship between injury numbers and rates in practice and competition is similar to previous findings (4). Competition injury rates were higher than practice injury rates, and more than five-fold higher for men's football and ice hockey. This difference might be attributable to a higher intensity of activity during competitions compared with practices; in most sports, the proportion of injuries requiring ≥7 days before return to full participation was higher in competitions than in practices. However, a larger number of injuries occurred during practices than competition, because there were nearly 4.5 times as many practice athlete-exposures as competition athlete-exposures. Approximately one in five practice injuries required ≥7 days before return to full participation. Major injuries, such as concussion or those resulting in surgery or emergency transport, occurred commonly in both competition and practice. Injury prevention strategies that target not only competition, but also the more controlled practice environment, might provide additional opportunities to reduce injury incidence.

The findings in this report are subject to at least four limitations. First, not all sports have athletic trainers present at every practice; therefore, practice and overall injury rates might be underreported and thus underestimated in certain sports. Second, these data are descriptive and cannot be used to ascertain reasons for the various injury rates. Third, multiple years of data were required to be combined to provide stable annual estimates. For methodologic reasons, it cannot be ascertained whether rates have changed over time. Additional years of injury surveillance will aid detection of changes in injury incidence and severity. Finally, although weights were used to calculate national rate estimates, these data are drawn from reports from participating teams, which amounts to a convenience sample and not a random sample. Thus, these data might not be generalizable to all teams in all NCAA member schools.

Sports injury data, such as those collected by NCAA-ISP, have been used to describe the incidence of injury, develop and evaluate various rule and policy changes (e.g., changing football kickoff and touchback yard lines to reduce injuries*), guide resource allocation, and focus injury prevention efforts (2,4–10). NCAA-ISP data are now available online to researchers to aid in their analyses of sports injuries and in their development of strategies for injury prevention.[†]

[1]Datalys Center for Sports Injury Research and Prevention, Indianapolis, Indiana; [2]University of North Carolina Injury Prevention Research Center, Chapel Hill; [3]State Health Registry of Iowa, Iowa City; [4]University of Maryland, College Park, Maryland; [5]Division of Unintentional Injury Prevention, National Center for Injury Prevention and Control, CDC.

References

1. National Collegiate Athletic Association. Sports sponsorship and participation rates. Indianapolis, IN: National Collegiate Athletic Association; 2014. Available at http://www.ncaa.org/about/resources/research/sports-sponsorship-and-participation-research.
2. Kerr ZY, Dompier TP, Snook EM, et al. National collegiate athletic association injury surveillance system: review of methods for 2004–2005 through 2013–2014 data collection. J Athl Train 2014;49:552–60.
3. Kucera KL, Marshall SW, Bell DR, DiStefano MJ, Goerger CP, Oyama S. Validity of soccer injury data from the National Collegiate Athletic Association's Injury Surveillance System. J Athl Train 2011;46:489–99.
4. Hootman JM, Dick R, Agel J. Epidemiology of collegiate injuries for 15 sports: summary and recommendations for injury prevention initiatives. J Athl Train 2007;42:311–9.
5. Gilchrist J, Mandelbaum B, Melancon H, et al. A randomized controlled trial to prevent non-contact ACL injury in female collegiate soccer players. Am J Sports Med 2008;36:1476–83.
6. Reider B. An ounce of prevention. Am J Sports Med 2004;32:1383–4.
7. Dick R, Putukian M, Agel J, Evans TA, Marshall SW. Descriptive epidemiology of collegiate women's soccer injuries: National Collegiate Athletic Association Injury Surveillance System, 1988–1989 through 2002–2003. J Athl Train 2007;42:278–85.
8. Marshall SW, Covassin T, Dick R, Nassar LG, Agel J. Descriptive epidemiology of collegiate women's gymnastics injuries: National Collegiate Athletic Association Injury Surveillance System, 1988–1989 through 2003–2004. J Athl Train 2007;42:234–40.
9. Yard EE, Comstock RD. Compliance with return to play guidelines following concussion in US high school athletes, 2005–2008. Brain Inj 2009;23:888–98.
10. Parker EM, Gilchrist J, Schuster D, Lee R, Sarmiento K. Reach and knowledge change among coaches and other participants of the online course: "concussion in sports: what you need to know." J Head Trauma Rehabil 2015;30:198–206.

* Additional information available at http://www.ncaa.org/about/resources/media-center/news/playing-rules-oversight-panel-approves-rules-changes-football.

† Additional information available at http://www.datalyscenter.org/index.php.

Summary

What is already known on this topic?

The risk for injury to college athletes varies by the sport played, the sex of the athlete, and whether the athlete is engaged in practice or competition.

What is added by this report?

Data from the National Collegiate Athletic Association Injury Surveillance Program indicate that, among men's sports, the highest injury rates are in football and wrestling. For women, the highest injury rates are in soccer and gymnastics. Estimated injury rates are higher during competition than during practice. However, the majority of injuries overall and within most sports occur during practices because they are conducted more frequently than competitions.

What are the implications for public health practice?

Injury prevention strategies that target practices as well as competitions might provide additional opportunities for reduction in injury incidence. Injury surveillance data can be used to compare injury incidence across sports, develop and evaluate rule and policy changes, and focus injury prevention research and programs. Continual analysis of surveillance data will help to understand changes in the incidence and severity of college sports injuries.

Print Citations

CMS: Kerr, Zachary Y., Stephen W. Marshall, Thomas P. Dompier, et al. "College Sports-Related Injuries—United States, 2009–10 through 2013–14 Academic Years." In *The Reference Shelf: College Sports,* edited by Micah L. Issitt, 80-85. Amenia, NY: Grey House Publishing, 2021.

MLA: Kerr, Zachary Y., Stephen W. Marshall, Thomas P. Dompier, et al. "College Sports-Related Injuries—United States, 2009–10 through 2013–14 Academic Years." *The Reference Shelf: College Sports,* edited by Micah L. Issitt, Grey House Publishing, 2021, pp. 80-85.

APA: Kerr, Z. Y., Marshall, S. W., & Dompier, T. P., et al. (2021). College sports-related injuries—United States, 2009–10 through 2013–14 academic years. In Micah L. Issitt (Ed.), *The reference shelf: College sports* (pp. 80-85). Amenia, NY: Grey House Publishing.

Poor Students More Likely to Play Football, Despite Brain Injury Concerns

By Amanda Morris and Michel Martin
NPR, February 3, 2019

Fears of brain injuries has deterred many parents and their children from choosing to play football.

After years of publicity about how dangerous football can be, football enrollment has declined 6.6 percent in the past decade, according to data from the National Federation of State High School Associations.

Those who still play the sport are increasingly low-income students.

Over the past five years in Illinois, the proportion of high school football rosters filled by low-income boys rose nearly 25 percent—even as the number of players in the state has fallen by 14.8 percent over the same period, according to a story out this week from HBO's *Real Sports*.

This doesn't surprise Albert Samaha, a *BuzzFeed News* investigative reporter and author of *Never Ran, Never Will: Boyhood and Football in a Changing American Inner City*.

Samaha spent two seasons embedded with the Mo Better Jaguar football program in Brownsville, a small Brooklyn neighborhood overburdened with poverty and crime. The program is for children ages 7-13, who are all aware of the risks of playing football, but play anyway.

"The reason that football is so valuable to them is the fact that it's still the sport that that's the most popular in America, that is getting the most money from high schools and colleges in America," Samaha said in an interview with NPR's Michel Martin on *All Things Considered*. "At a time when the educational gap continues to widen between low income, particularly black and brown kids, and higher income white kids, football offers a path to upward mobility that is not really available through any other extracurricular activity."

Many of the 10, 11, and 12-year olds who Samaha reported on told him that they were playing football not just for the chance of getting a college scholarship, but also for the chance to get financial aid for top private high schools in New York City.

Their hopes were reinforced by private high school coaches who attended Mo Better Jaguar football games and told the boys that if they played well enough, they could get a scholarship, and with that scholarship, avoid the student debt and poverty that so many in generations before them faced.

"Kids feel pressured to play football, it's rooted in the problem of education," Samaha said.

So why do so many low-income students choose football, and not a different, less dangerous, sport? Why not try for a baseball scholarship? Or soccer?

It's a numbers game.

The odds of getting a college scholarship for a man playing football at a NCAA or NAIA school is 43:1, according to *MarketWatch*, and football offers far more athletic scholarships at NCAA and NAIA schools than any other sport, numbering close to 26,000 per year.

At the high school level, schools are investing big money into football as well. One high school in Katy, Texas, just outside of Houston, recently spent over 70 million dollars on a new state-of-the-art football stadium.

"As long as the money is going into this activity this is where the opportunities are going to be," Samaha said.

Additionally, unlike some sports, football has a relatively low barrier of entry of participation, because there are so many positions that rely on differing capabilities.

"Football unlike other sports doesn't require you to be a certain size or certain height," Samaha said. "You can sort of play it whether you're overweight whether you're underweight. It's sort of the most in some ways meritocratic of all the sports available for these opportunities."

But with the opportunity to achieve affordable higher education, playing football also brings the risk of long-term brain damage.

A report by the Journal of the American Medical Association, published in 2017, showed that in a study of 111 brains of deceased former National Football League players, 110 had evidence of chronic traumatic encephalopathy (CTE).

CTE has been linked with repeated blows to the head, and can result in behavioral changes and cognitive decline.

Some of the behavioral side effects include difficulty with impulse control, aggression, emotional volatility and rage behavior. Extensive signs of CTE has been found in the brains of former NFL stars such as former New England Patriots tight end Aaron Hernandez, who hung himself in a prison cell while serving a life sentence for murder.

It's not just NFL players though. The same study showed that in the 202 brains examined across all levels of play, nearly 88 percent of all the brains, 177, had CTE.

Playing football is still worth the risk, because they're trying to avoid other dangers.

Low-income students who choose to play football know about these risks, Samaha said, but have factored it into a bigger risk assessment calculation. For them, playing football is still worth the risk, because they're trying to avoid other dangers.

"It's a luxury to worry about these long-term, sort of abstract damages to these kids and their parents," Samaha said. "The risks are all around them—the risks of not going to high school, the risks of not making it into college, or the risks of falling into kind of the street path that they'd seen other people around them fall into."

Football is their ticket out. But Samaha argues that America needs to reckon with the broader ethical implications of the sport.

"America's dual commitments to football and racial oppression have meant that the danger of the sport will increasingly fall on the shoulders of low income black and brown kids," Samaha said.

Meanwhile, he says, the money from the sport is mainly going to white coaches and white owners.

Samaha likened the disparity between the people who participate in football and the people who benefit to a "gladiatorial dichotomy."

Meanwhile, there has been no real decline in viewership for the sport. A 2017 Gallup poll showed that football still leads as America's favorite sport, with 37 percent of U.S. adults choosing it as their favorite sport to watch.

Millions are expected to watch the Super Bowl on Sunday, including Samaha.

"I feel guilty about it but I watch every Sunday," he said. "I don't know how to reckon with that."

Sunday night, as millions look on, the players will inevitably clash in tangled lines of bodies on the field, perhaps risking a lot for a few yards—risking more to win.

Print Citations

CMS: Morris, Amanda, and Michel Martin. "Poor Students More Likely to Play Football, Despite Brain Injury Concerns." In *The Reference Shelf: College Sports,* edited by Micah L. Issitt, 86-88. Amenia, NY: Grey House Publishing, 2021.

MLA: Morris, Amanda, and Michel Martin. "Poor Students More Likely to Play Football, Despite Brain Injury Concerns." *The Reference Shelf: College Sports,* edited by Micah L. Issitt, Grey House Publishing, 2021, pp. 86-88.

APA: Morris, A., & Martin, M. (2021). Poor students more likely to play football, despite brain injury concerns. In Micah L. Issitt (Ed.), *The reference shelf: College sports* (pp. 86-88). Amenia, NY: Grey House Publishing.

College Athletes Show Signs of Possible Heart Injury after COVID-19

By Aimee Cunningham
ScienceNews, September 11, 2020

Amid growing concerns that a bout of COVID-19 might damage the heart, a small study is reporting signs of an inflammatory heart condition in college athletes who had the infection.

More than two dozen male and female competitive athletes underwent magnetic resonance imaging of their hearts in the weeks to months after a positive test for SARS-CoV-2, the virus that causes COVID-19. The images indicated swelling in the heart muscle and possible injury to cells in four of the athletes, or 15 percent, researchers report online September 11 in *JAMA Cardiology*. That could mean the athletes had myocarditis, an inflammation of the heart muscle most frequently caused by viral infections.

Heart images of eight additional athletes showed signs of possible injury to cells without evidence of swelling. It's more difficult to interpret whether these changes in the heart tissue are due to coronavirus infection, says Saurabh Rajpal, a cardiologist at the Ohio State University Wexner Medical Center in Columbus. One limitation of the research is the lack of images of the athletes' hearts prior to the illness for comparison, Rajpal and his colleagues write.

None of the 26 athletes in the study, who play football, soccer, basketball, lacrosse or run track, were hospitalized due to COVID-19. Twelve of the 26, including two of the four with signs of inflamed hearts, reported mild symptoms during their infection, such as fever, sore throat, muscle aches and difficulty breathing.

It will take more research to confirm the study's findings and understand what they could mean for these young hearts. For now, the results suggest the heart may be at risk of injury, and serve as a reminder that after having COVID-19—even with mild or no symptoms—young people need to pay close attention to how they are feeling when they return to exercise, says Rajpal. If they have symptoms like chest pain, shortness of breath or an abnormal heart beat, he says, they should see a doctor.

It's been apparent since early in the pandemic that COVID-19 can be worse in patients who already have heart problems (SN: 3/20/20). More recently, studies have reported on what the infection might do to the heart. For example, researchers assessed 100 German adult patients who'd recovered from COVID-19, one third of whom needed to be hospitalized. Cardiac MRIs revealed signs of heart inflammation in 60 of these patients after their infection.

Those signals of heart inflammation could mean that the patients had developed myocarditis, which is estimated to occur in approximately 22 out of 100,000 people annually around the world. Patients with myocarditis can experience chest pain, shortness of breath, fatigue or a rapid or irregular heartbeat. The heart can recover from myocarditis, but in rare cases, the condition can damage the heart muscle enough to lead to heart failure.

Bottom of Form

For athletes diagnosed with myocarditis, the recommendation is to stop participating in sports for three to six months to give the heart time to heal, as animal evidence suggests that vigorous exercise when the heart is still inflamed worsens the injury. With a break from sports, young athletes can expect to recover from myocarditis. But the condition is taken seriously: A 2015 study estimated that 10 percent of sudden cardiac deaths in NCAA athletes were due to myocarditis. When the Big Ten Conference, which includes Ohio State, announced in August that it was postponing its football season, one of the reported reasons was concerns about COVID-related myocarditis.

This new study of college athletes and COVID-19 "is really a step in the right direction," says Meagan Wasfy, a sports cardiologist at Massachusetts General Hospital. "We need more data like this." But it's hard to draw firm conclusions from the findings, she says. Cardiac MRI usually is used to confirm a diagnosis of myocarditis in combination with other clinical signs, including symptoms, blood test results that signal inflammation, high levels of a protein called troponin I that indicates stress on the heart and abnormal findings in an electrocardiogram.

In the study, while some athletes had signs of possible myocarditis in imaging, their troponin I levels were normal, and their electrocardiograms didn't look unusual. Wasfy sees a few possible explanations. Had the athletes been tested when they were first infected, those other clinical signs might have shown up. Perhaps the other indications had returned to normal by the time the cardiac MRI and other tests were performed. In that case, the MRI is a "ghost" of that prior inflammation and stress, she says.

> The heart may be at risk of injury, and serve as a reminder that after having COVID-19—even with mild or no symptoms—young people need to pay attention to how they are feeling when they return to exercise.

Another possibility is that SARS-CoV-2 is impacting the heart muscle in a way that cardiologists aren't accustomed to, absent some of the usual signs of inflammation and stress. Without those indicators of myocarditis, it's hard to say if the heart had this condition, she says.

Some might argue that the imaging signs could be chalked up to differences between the hearts of competitive athletes and those of the more sedentary. Wasfy thinks that's less likely, but cardiologists "certainly have a lot of work to do to define what the prevalence of these [imaging] findings is at baseline" in healthy athletes.

To expand on the study, Rajpal and his colleagues plan to take heart scans of more athletes, repeat cardiac MRIs in the athletes already imaged, and scan athletes who did not have COVID-19 to compare their images with those who have.

Print Citations

CMS: Cunningham, Aimee. "College Athletes Show Signs of Possible Heart Injury after COVID-19." In *The Reference Shelf: College Sports,* edited by Micah L. Issitt, 89-91. Amenia, NY: Grey House Publishing, 2021.

MLA: Cunningham, Aimee. "College Athletes Show Signs of Possible Heart Injury after COVID-19." *The Reference Shelf: College Sports,* edited by Micah L. Issitt, Grey House Publishing, 2021, pp. 89-91.

APA: Cunningham, A. (2021). College athletes show signs of possible heart injury after COVID-19. In Micah L. Issitt (Ed.), *The reference shelf: College sports* (pp. 89-91). Amenia, NY: Grey House Publishing.

College Football on the Brink: Push to Play Undercut by Virus Outbreaks

By Juan Perez Jr.
Politico, June 22, 2020

Colleges are racing toward a fall sports season unlike any other, as they work to keep the coronavirus from infecting student athletes and staff who bring in billions of dollars and entertain a nation.

So far, it's not going well.

Clemson University's athletics department disclosed 28 positive coronavirus tests among student athletes and staff on Friday, one day after the South Carolina state epidemiologist warned residents to wear masks in public and stay physically distanced from others. A group of Texas football players tested positive, as a stubborn number of cases persists in the state. Kansas State University suspended its ongoing football workouts for two weeks, after revealing 14 of about 130 student-athletes tested positive. "Make no mistake, we are not out of the woods yet," Kansas Gov. Laura Kelly said last week.

Across the country, college athletic programs are under financial and political pressure to return to the fields, but these efforts come amid safety warnings from public health officials and continued uncertainty about how the academic side of colleges will get back to business this fall. President Donald Trump may want to refill arenas to give Americans a sense of life returning to normal with sporting pastimes, but each positive test in an athletic clubhouse is a major setback.

"The decision should not be an economic decision," said Amy Perko, CEO of the Knight Commission college sports reform group, of the potential to restart competition this fall. "Leaders should not rush to a return just to meet a date on the traditional (sports) schedule."

Three months after Covid-19 halted March Madness basketball tournaments, college leaders are wading through evolving information about the disease and its ability to spread through contact sports. They're also asking Congress for protection from legal liability.

But as states reopen, lockdowns lift and infections smolder in some states, the prospect of a virus-tinged sports season underscores broader tensions between safety and money. Health experts are urging administrators to craft intricate campus safety plans, while college towns rely on the economic activity generated by fall

Saturdays. How colleges proceed will send a message about the influence of athletics—and the cash produced by big-time programs—in higher education.

NCAA and college football playoff officials huddled with the Trump administration and professional leagues in April to discuss Covid-19 testing and Centers for Disease Control and Prevention guidelines. Last week, a panel of the athletic overseer's authorities allowed Division I schools to start required football activities in mid-July in preparation for scheduled Labor Day weekend kickoffs.

Top-tier fall college championships can run on their usual formats, timelines and locations. Division II schools are also holding to their plans, at least for now.

Yet there are still no hard rules on what happens to a player who tests positive during the season, or the rest of the team. How to travel safely is another problem. The CDC has urged higher education institutions to limit activities involving "external groups or organizations," especially those that include people from outside communities.

College athletes are unpaid and nonunionized students who live in close contact with their peers, though they are often portrayed like professional stars. Black students accounted for just 10 percent of the student body at Division I schools in 2019, according to NCAA statistics, but Black athletes occupied nearly half the ranks of those top-grossing schools' football teams.

At big-time sports programs, those same youths generate an outsized chunk of business income through television broadcasts, ticket sales and sports bar tabs.

Public school sports programs in the NCAA's highest-profile Football Bowl Subdivision generated roughly $8.8 billion in revenue in 2018. A lucrative cash flow combination delivered more than half of those dollars. That includes media rights deals, ticket sales, revenue-sharing agreements with athletic conferences and the NCAA, plus postseason football games and sponsorships.

> College athletes are unpaid and nonunionized students live in close contact with their peers, though they are often portrayed like professional stars.

The money helps pay for some of the biggest-ticket expenses associated with college sports. According to aggregate data maintained by the Knight Commission, public Football Bowl Subdivision schools spent $5 billion—nearly 60 percent of their total expenses in 2018—on salaries and benefits for coaches and staff, in addition to overhead costs such as debt service on athletics facilities projects and equipment.

Less income means less money to pay salaries or service debt. Other teams must brace for hits to crucial support that in the past came from college budgets now reeling from pandemic-spurred losses.

Stamping out potential campus outbreaks hinges on testing for Covid-19, plus isolating the infected and tracing their contacts. Yet some athletic conferences and schools are still building clear, consistent and definitive standards to test athletes for the disease in the coming weeks and months.

Others have uneven plans for how they'll acquire tests, which kind they will administer and when—or how much they will cost.

"Everybody has major questions. We may do a lot of testing and have major outbreaks, we may do very little testing and have no outbreaks," said Carlos Del Rio, the executive associate dean of the Emory School of Medicine and a member of an NCAA coronavirus advisory committee.

Recent NCAA guidance doesn't offer schools specific answers to those difficult questions.

"University athletic departments can put together safe venues—they're used to reducing infections in locker rooms," said Rep. Donna Shalala (D-Fla.), a former university administrator, during a recent panel discussion.

"Here's the problem: You're dealing with a bunch of young people that are going to socialize. So, while you can control training, locker rooms, [and] playing venues, what you can't control is the rest of what it means to be young in America. That's the challenge. That's why testing, particularly quick testing, is going to be extremely important."

That has created some tough decisions. Arizona State's president says his teams might only compete with schools inside the Pac-12 Conference in the western United States this year.

"I don't know if we'll be playing teams from other conferences or not, but I think we can make the conference work. That's basically what we're headed towards," ASU President Michael Crow told *Politico*. "I'd say that it's becoming increasingly likely, and we're putting all of our energy into making that happen."

Some schools simply may not play at all.

"One possibility is that at some point in time, people may say this is not safe no matter what we do, we can never make it safe enough, and therefore we shouldn't have sports," del Rio said.

"I think schools, parents, and athletes are going to have to decide, 'Is this a risk I can take?'"

Three University of Central Florida football players tested positive for Covid-19 upon returning to the Orlando campus for workouts earlier this month. Student athletes and an employee tested positive at Marshall University, while other athlete infections were reported at Alabama, Iowa State, Oklahoma State, Louisiana State, Mississippi, Texas Tech and other schools.

"I think what you try to do is try to minimize the risk as much as you can," del Rio said. "But obviously it's going to be impossible to say (there's) zero risk."

One problem is getting testing for everyone on campus who needs it.

For example, if all of Connecticut's colleges and boarding schools reopen in the fall, higher education officials have estimated the state needs to provide 200,000 to 300,000 Covid-19 tests by early September—plus more for the remaining fall semester. A report from Mississippi's public university system says schools need to ask the state's health department "to provide massive testing and contact tracing capabilities."

The American College Health Association says repeated testing is needed to assure a population "remains clear of disease," but cautions mass testing programs require immense resources and close coordination with health officials to avoid overwhelming labs or health care workers.

Testing all members of a sports team before a tournament could be feasible, the association said early this month, but argued testing even for both Covid-19 infections and immunity "cannot provide a comprehensive picture of the safety of the student athlete 'herd.'"

"The question of COVID-19 testing of intercollegiate athletes or other at-risk groups has not yet been settled and is controversial," the college health association said. "There will also be questions about the need for repeated testing and how often."

Among schools, plans are in flux.

The University System of Georgia is reviewing coronavirus response plans from its individual schools but is still weighing critical details on how campus testing will work.

Interim guidelines from the Pac-12 Conference call for testing athletes before they return to campus, but a spokesperson said officials are still discussing critical details including testing frequency.

Ohio State says its athletes must get tested before they return to voluntary workouts this month, yet the school didn't specify estimates on how many tests will be needed as practices and competitions resume. Plans from the University of Kansas and Texas Tech call for athletes to get a diagnostic and antibody test before starting workouts, while Oklahoma State has said repeat testing will depend on guidance from medical professionals, the Big 12 Conference and the NCAA.

To get more answers, del Rio said experts will need to know more about how the virus behaves in the coming two months.

"I think the risk for athletes is probably going to be very small because they're young and they're going to do fine," del Rio said.

"But I worry about coaches, I worry about the other people that are with the athletes, who are not necessarily young and who are not necessarily in good health," he said. "And that may be a problem."

Print Citations

CMS: Perez, Jr., Juan. "College Football on the Brink: Push to Play Undercut by Virus Outbreaks." In *The Reference Shelf: College Sports,* edited by Micah L. Issitt, 92-95. Amenia, NY: Grey House Publishing, 2021.

MLA: Perez, Jr., Juan. "College Football on the Brink: Push to Play Undercut by Virus Outbreaks." *The Reference Shelf: College Sports,* edited by Micah L. Issitt, Grey House Publishing, 2021, pp. 92-95.

APA: Perez, Jr., J. (2021). College football on the brink: Push to play undercut by virus outbreaks. In Micah L. Issitt (Ed.), *The reference shelf: College sports* (pp. 92-95). Amenia, NY: Grey House Publishing.

4
Access to Athletics

Bailar—the first openly transgender NCAA Division I swimmer—speaking at a 2017 Pride conference.

Race and Gender in Collegiate Athletics

One of the issues in collegiate athletics has been the struggle for fairness and equality. At one time in US history, only white males could compete. The field was eventually opened to white women, and gradually to people of color. Despite this progress, there are still challenges in terms of diversity and representation. The entire field of competitive sports is changing due to new questions regarding the status of trans athletes at both the college and professional levels.

Race and Collegiate Sports

A cursory look at collegiate sports in 2021 might seem to indicate that color barriers have been broken and that athletes of color enjoy the same access to athletic opportunities as any white student. For most of American history people of color were not accepted in the world of organized athletics. Prior to the 1950s, segregation laws meant that most people of color were prohibited from playing collegiate sports in mixed-race teams. This remained the case until well into the twentieth century, with local and state laws prohibiting black athletes from playing games with white athletes. While not specific to collegiate athletics, these laws limited the involvement of athletes of color in professional and amateur athletics. Black athletes of any age could still "negro leagues," but they were largely barred from participating in the mainstream collegiate or professional leagues.

Informal rules and prejudice meant that athletes of color could not join in collegiate sport even in schools with no specific rules prohibiting their involvement. Black athletes were also accepted in some northern states long before they were embraced in southern schools or professional teams. Teams that had black athletes would keep them off their playing rosters when visiting the South. A famous instance of this happened in 1916, when Rutgers University kept Paul Robeson—who went on to become an American entertainment and civil rights icon—off the field because the opposing team, Washington and Lee College, refused to play otherwise.

More than any other factor, the growth in the popularity of college sports after World War II, pushed integration of collegiate teams. With increasing pressure to build winning franchises that could earn increasingly lucrative revenues, colleges began recruiting athletes of color even though there was significant social reluctance to integration. Historian Timothy Davis, in his article "The Myth of the Superspade," argues that integration only came to sports that earned significant revenues and thus that integration was exploitative at the onset.[1]

Over the years, activism and changing cultural standards brought people of color into collegiate sports in far higher numbers, but players of color still face racism and prejudice. In addition to overt forms of racism and discrimination, athletes of color are also exploited because of structural and institutionalized racism in the way that the benefits of collegiate sports are distributed.

As of 2021, black players play an essential role in the two highest revenue-earning men's sports, basketball and football, and yet little of the revenue from these sports filters back into black communities. A 2020 study from the National Bureau of Economic Research (NBER) looked at the distribution of profit from collegiate sports and found that students who are predominantly white and come from upper-class neighborhoods enjoy most of the benefit from collegiate athletics profits. Revenues from college sports subsidize resources that are most often utilized by white students and their families. The authors argue that this means that players of color are being exploited by a system that monetizes their effort and skill but does not compensate them, returning little revenue to athletes of color, their families, or their communities.[2]

The Gender Lines

In the United States, women have long been prohibited from taking part in professional sports because of sexism and misogyny, and in the past arguments have been put forth that playing sports was dangerous for women because of the physiological demands of menstruation or child birth.

Despite these efforts to keep women out of sports, women's leagues and groups organized and played their own games. There were informal sporting leagues in many major cities in the early 1900s, with women playing games like archery, tennis, croquet, and bowling, though few women engaged in games that were still stereotypically considered part of the male domain, like football, soccer, or baseball. Women's basketball was first introduced at Smith College in 1892 and spread to other colleges in the next decade. Women athletes wanted to compete with athletes from other institutions but this was considered inappropriate. The first extramural women's sports competitions at the collegiate level took place in 1896, between women's basketball teams from California and Washington.[3]

The feminist movement of the 1920s began to change things in women's sports, with more and more colleges investing in women's teams and holding competitions, but progress stalled during the Great Depression, as did women's enrollment in colleges and universities. The situation changed during World War II when, with so many men overseas and drafted into the military, women were called upon to play a more direct role in professions that had previously been reserved for men. Organized as a substitute for men's teams because of the war, the All-American Girls Baseball League (formed in 1943) was one of the first professional women's sports teams, paving the way for a much higher level of interest in sports among women of all ages. By the 1950s, this led to more and more women taking an interest in collegiate sports.

Women's rights took center stage during the civil rights movement of the 1950s and 60s, and women athletes protested the policies that kept them out of organized athletics. The 1967 Association for Intercollegiate Athletics for Women (AIAW) and other organizations pushed for colleges and universities to invest in women's sports. The primary victory was the passage of Title IX of the Education Amendments of 1972, which prohibits gender discrimination in educational institutions. Colleges and universities receiving federal support or funding cannot discriminate against student athletes and must, under the law, provide opportunities for women to take part in sports. This provided a framework within which students could challenge the allocation of funds provided for athletics programs and could request or promote the expansion of women's sports opportunities.

In the twenty-first century, 40 percent of all participants in college or professional sports are female, and yet women's sports receive only a fraction of the funding and media attention directed at male sports teams. Investment in male sports teams is around two and a half times higher than in women's sports. This contrasts with the vast increase in interest among young women. One of the reasons for this disparity lies with NCAA management. Prior to women being included in the NCAA, the AIAW was still the managing body for women's collegiate athletics, and this organization had a more direct focus on the welfare and resources afforded to women's athletes. Members of the governing board were women and so had a personal investment in the issue. In 1978, universities and colleges were forced to comply with Title IX and when this occurred, the NCAA launched a legal effort to take over women's sports. They won this contest in court, essentially dissolving the AIAW and bringing women's collegiate sports under the auspices of the NCAA. This organization, dominated by males and focused predominantly on male athletics, reduced investment in women's teams.[4]

Over the past 50 years, interest in athletics among women has grown significantly. Women now constitute nearly 50 percent of the market for sports and fitness equipment and interest in competitive athletics at the high school and collegiate level has increased markedly since the 1990s. The potential for growth in women's sports now outpaces the potential for growth in men's sports, such that analysts now argue that women's sports might be key to future sports revenues and more lucrative for potential investment.[5]

Critics argue that sexism continues to be a major factor in how women's sports are viewed. They argue that colleges and universities treat investment in women's sports as a burden or an additional cost. Many also point out that mainstream media devotes only 4 percent of coverage to women's sports despite women athletes constituting more than 44 percent of the sports audience. Economic pressure to improve women's sports, to promote women's sports contests and to support women athletes is likely to intensify in the future.

The Question of Gender

By far the biggest debate in the arena of access to sports in the 2010s and 20s involves whether or not trans athletes should be allowed to compete in leagues representing their gender identity or should be restricted to participating in leagues representing their assigned sex at birth. This is only one of the many arenas of American culture in which analysts and the public are struggling to come to grips with trans individuals.

Trans advocates argue that a person should be afforded the right to participate in society according to their gender identity rather than their sex at birth. From this perspective, trans women are women and should be allowed to participate in society as women, including on women's sports teams. This creates a problem, however, in the world of athletics. A trans woman might have a body type influenced by hormones that are typically associated with the male sex and so may develop musculature that cisgender women (women who identify as women and are assigned female sex at birth) cannot develop because they lack the chemical precursors. Individuals born into the male sex have, for instance, 75 percent more muscle mass and 90 percent more upper body strength than females. A trans woman therefore might have what some consider an unfair advantage when competing against women who are born into the female sex. This same argument might hold that it is also unfair for a trans woman to compete against a trans man, who is a man who is born into the female sex and so has outward female sex characteristics.[6]

This raises questions about whether or not gender is an appropriate way to classify people for the purposes of sports competition. Imagine, for instance, if participating in sports was based on a physical characteristic not related to the construct of gender, such as muscle mass. If sports were organized in this way, then individuals applying to play on a team would fall into certain classes based on average muscle mass, weight, height, etc. Organized in this way, all sports would be "co-ed" because the divisions would be based on body type rather than conflating body type and gender.

Of course, reorganizing all of sports into new categories may appear unrealistic and impossible to achieve, but it is an interesting thought experiment when engaging in the debate over trans participation in sports, whether at the collegiate or the professional level.

Works Used

Bell, Richard C. "A History of Women in Sport Prior to Title IX." *The Sport Journal*. https://thesportjournal.org/article/a-history-of-women-in-sport-prior-to-title-ix/. Accessed 18 May 2021.

Davis, Timothy. "The Myth of the Superspade: The Persistence of Racism in College Athletics." *Fordham Urban Law Journal*. Vol. 22, No. 3 (1995). https://ir.lawnet.fordham.edu/cgi/viewcontent.cgi?article=1664&context=ulj&httpsredir=1&referer=. Accessed 18 May 2021.

Garthwaite, Criag, Jordan Keener, Matthew J. Notowidigdo, and Nicole F. Ozminkowski. "Who Profits from Amateurism? Rent-Sharing in Modern College Sports." *NBER*. Working Paper 27734. August 2020. https://www.nber.org/system/files/working_papers/w27734/w27734.pdf. Accessed 19 May 2021.

Higgins, Laine. "Women's College Sports Was Growing: Then the NCAA Took

Over." *The Wall Street Journal*. Apr 3, 2021. https://www.wsj.com/articles/women-college-sports-ncaa-aiaw-11617422325. Accessed 18 May 2021.

Strauss, Ben, and Molly Hensley-Clancy. "Women's Sports Can Do at Least One Thing Men's Can't, Experts Say: Get Bigger." *The Washington Post*. Apr 1, 2021. https://www.washingtonpost.com/sports/2021/04/01/womens-sports-growth-ratings-business/. Accessed 19 May 2021.

"Why Males Pack a Powerful Punch." *Science Daily*. Feb 5, 2020. https://www.sciencedaily.com/releases/2020/02/200205132404.htm#:~:text=It's%20already%20known%20that%20males,%25%20more%20strength%20than%20females'. Accessed 25 May 2021.

Notes

1. Davis, "The Myth of the Superspade: The Persistence of Racism in College Athletics."
2. Garthwaite, Keener, Notowidigdo, Ozminkowski, "Who Profits from Amateurism? Rent-Sharing in Modern College Sports."
3. Bell, "A History of Women in Sport Prior to Title IX."
4. Higgins, "Women's College Sports Was Growing: Then the NCAA Took Over."
5. Strauss and Hensley-Clancy, "Women's Sports Can Do at Least One Thing Men's Can't, Experts Say: Get Bigger."
6. "Why Males Pack a Powerful Punch," *Science Daily*.

"I Signed My Life Away to Rich White Guys": Athletes on the Racial Dynamics of College Sports

By Nathan Kalman-Lamb, Derek Silva, and Johanna Mellis
The Guardian, March 17, 2021

On 30 January, Rutgers basketball player Geo Baker wrote on Instagram in response to a post by US college sports' governing body, the NCAA: "I have to sign a paper that says my name and likeness belongs to the school. Modern day slavery. u realize we are playing in a pandemic being told to stay away from everyone we love just for y'all entertainment but i can't sell my own jersey with my last name on it to help my future financially. That makes sense to u?" In invoking "slavery" and linking it to both the denial of economic rights for US college athletes–or, to call them what they really are, campus athletic workers–and the ongoing requirement of play during a pandemic, Baker highlights one of the ugliest dimensions of the college sport industrial complex: the disproportionately racialized nature of its exploitative dynamics.

This week marks the start of the biggest event on the college sports calendar, the NCAA Basketball Tournament. And for those unfamiliar with the absurdist world of US college sports, it is big business. Like, *really* big business, particularly in the elite Power Five conferences. How big? In the 2018-2019 academic year, the 65 Power Five universities generated $8.3bn through athletics. Yet, aside from scholarships, players don't see any of that money directly. If players did receive a share, economist David Berri has calculated that men's basketball players at an elite Power Five school like Duke would receive between $145,000 and $4.13m per year. And, here's the thing: an extremely high proportion of the players being systematically denied the revenue they are responsible for generating are Black.

Based on the NCAA's own figures, at the predominantly white institutions (PWIs) that comprise the Power Five, as of the 2019-2020 season, Black students comprise only 5.7% of the population. Yet, in the Power Five, Black athletes make up 55.9% of men's basketball players, 55.7% of men's football, and 48.1% of women's basketball. At some schools, the numbers are particularly startling. Texas A&M, the second-highest athletic revenue earning institution in US college sports, has only 3.1% Black students in the general student body. Yet, its college football team is 75% Black, and its women's basketball team 92.9%. It is hard to deny from these numbers that Black athletes are admitted into institutions that usually ignore them specifically to have their labor exploited for the universities' gain.

These numbers are all the more galling given recent events. When Texas Longhorns football players did not remain on the field during the singing of "The Eyes of Texas" this fall because of what they called the song's "racial undertones," wealthy alumni threatened to pull donations and spammed the university with racist vitriol. One particularly troubling email sent by donor Larry Wilkinson read "less than 6% of our current study body is black...the tail cannot be allowed to wag the dog.... and the dog must instead stand up for what is right. Nothing forces those students to attend UT Austin. Encourage them to select an alternate school...NOW!" As a consequence of these letters, players were told that if they did not participate, they could lose access to job opportunities after graduating.

More recently, Creighton men's basketball head coach Greg McDermott admitted that he demanded players "stay on the plantation" during a postgame talk. Although he claimed to have offered to resign, the university chose not to take him up on the offer, presumably due to the success of his tenure. Meanwhile, in Tennessee, GOP state law-makers called on universities across the state to prohibit athletes from engaging in anti-racist protests during the national anthem. Each of these incidents offers us just a hint of the too-often veiled racist climate Black athletes must endure on campuses across the country.

Former University of Wisconsin men's basketball star Nigel Hayes explains, "It's always been an interesting situation and dynamic. Black athletes, but white school, white coaches, white fans... minimal Black people." Hayes, who briefly played in the NBA and currently plays professionally in Europe, adds: "Most are aware these university teams, primarily men's basketball and football, are filled with Black players. Making money for usually white people

> **It is impossible to fully grasp the nature of these exploitative dynamics without viewing them within the broader context of racial capitalism.**

and not being able to have their share of a billion dollar plus industry. So the visual you get is white institutions recruit Black talent to make millions. While dealing with all the other hurdles of being Black."

We spoke to a number of current or recently graduated players about the racist dimensions of their experiences at Power Five PWIs. Most athletes were granted anonymity given the potential for reprisal from their colleges or employers.

Hayes's sentiment was echoed by Paul, a former SEC men's basketball player: "Every time I signed that piece of paper that said my name and likeness belonged to [university], I felt like I was giving up a piece of myself. Why should my school own my name? My image? How is that fair? I am a grown man. A Black man. And I have to sign my life away to who? To a bunch of rich white guys."

The most recent data available from the NCAA (the 2018-2019 season) makes it clear that the primary beneficiaries of college sport are white. Although non-Hispanic/Latino white people make 60.1% of the US population, 84.4% of Power Five chancellors and presidents are white. In athletic departments across the Power Five, 75% of athletic directors. At the coaching level, 80.6% of head men's basketball coaches, 81.54% of head women's basketball coaches, and 80% of head football coaches in the Power Five are white. Why does this matter? The enormous revenue generated by Power Five sports subsidizes the salaries of white individuals in leadership roles despite the enormous pool of Black candidates for those jobs.

Former NBA player David West puts it this way: "Athletes are expected to be content as an unpaid labor force for a system that allows economic opportunities for everyone but [them]. The racial undertones are always there."

It is not only the schools and their well-paid leadership that benefit from this unpaid labor. The college sport industrial complex also subsidizes major media corporations and the journalists who staff them. According to the Institute for Diversity and Ethics in Sport, 85% of sports editors and 82.1% of sports reporters are white. Pre-pandemic, CBS/Turner pulled in at least $655.1m from the men's basketball NCAA Tournament alone, while ESPN networks earned $792.5m in ad revenue from college football. This revenue is entirely predicated on the racialized labor of unpaid campus athletic workers largely at Power Five schools.

It is impossible to fully grasp the nature of these exploitative dynamics without viewing them within the broader context of racial capitalism, the concept made famous by Cedric Robinson, which is to say global histories of colonialism and capitalism build to systematically extract wealth from people of color. Precisely because of the violent and systematic exploitation of unfree labor that built the United States, there exists what we might call a racialized political economy of life chances one that distributes opportunity and access in massively unequal ways, particularly between white and Black Americans. This is how racial capitalism functions as a form of coercion.

If a scholarship and chance to play college sport is one of the best possibilities available for material uplift, it is something of a no-brainer to take that opportunity. But, when a choice is between bad and worse, then it isn't really freely made—and that is exactly what we are talking about in the context of college sports. How else do we explain McDermott's instinctive use of the plantation analogy? McDermott's repulsive comments should not be dismissed as one-off lapses of judgement, but part and parcel of what Billy Hawkins calls "the new plantation": a structure that views Black bodies as expendable and their labor essentially exploitable.

Guardian columnist and former NBA player Etan Thomas explains the impossibility of authentic consent in a neocolonial context this way: "You know when a company goes into an underdeveloped country and sets up shop there, and hires the locals there for pennies while the company makes billions of dollars. Then pretends that they are doing the locals a favor by providing a job opportunity for them that they otherwise wouldn't have, and [provides] other benefits—maybe food and clothes and some form of healthcare—so they can stay healthy enough to continue working. That's basically the system the NCAA has."

Joe, an ACC football player, in reflecting on Black athletes working for PWIs, immediately picked up on the fictitious notion that participation equates to consent: "It is a dynamic we are kind of forced not to think about in my opinion. For me football was always used as a ticket or a way out of the way I was living. Therefore, I feel as though I was never able to address the fact that people don't care about me but only my athletic ability. It is especially hard doing it for no compensation that is worth what we have to endure both mentally and physically. It is kind of like slave owner Mandingo fighter, in that my coach is measured on how good his slaves perform. I even had a white woman tell me I 'better be careful, *boy*,' cause I was going south. All in all I don't think everyone in my community was like this. I just feel as though I was looked at and treated a certain way and did not have the same opportunities as some of my teammates due to my skin color."

Similarly, Marla, a current WNBA player, shed light on the unique challenges faced by Black women in this context: "As a Black woman, the dynamics I experienced while I was at school were different. Yeah, of course we felt that we had no choice but to do what they told us and that our time wasn't ours until basketball was done, not even when it came to school. But there was also this constant need for us to justify our existence compared to the guys. Everything for us was much harder to get credit for, even if we won more games."

Jordan M Fields, a former track athlete at Pittsburgh, told us that "the extreme power imbalance that exists between Black college athletes, and white athletic administrators and coaches was obvious to me."

Like Joe, she ultimately viewed college sport through the prism of the plantation: "College athletic programs rely on Black athletes' labor and increase their profit the more they exploit them physically and restrict their academic and social freedom. My comparisons of sports at the college level, to the plantation system, focus on the 'plantation' not necessarily as a place, but as the extremely self-degrading and manipulated mindset of countless Black athletes caused by their exploitation and the undermining of their personal and professional growth as young Black men and women. I never had the opportunity to speak freely amongst other athletes at my alma mater about this, and I don't believe the conversation would've been welcomed amongst athletic department leadership."

This position was shared by another current ACC football player: "Recently, especially this last 2020 season, you could see the slave mentality some have regarding athletes. If you're producing there is no problem, but however you show or express any concern outside of football or your respective sport, you're a 'liability.'"

Andrew, a SEC football player, highlighted how the NCAA's prohibition on earnings have consequences for Black players, who are often denied the social capital that accrues to white athletes from college sport.

"While the education is great, being a minority and an athlete disadvantages you from being able to take full advantage of the opportunity. I was told by coaches to drop classes that would take up too much time. I was told that my GPA was fine as long as my eligibility wasn't at risk. To have a lack of support from the athletic side, and to not be able to fulfill my academic potential is tough.

"The system isn't fair, and many seem to think it's broken. The truth is that it's working as intended. The majority of scholarship athletes who are Black struggle to find good paying jobs out of college if they can't make it [to the NFL], while white players, walk on or not, often land jobs at least earning $60,000 a year. This isn't a coincidence, I've witnessed first hand the difference in experience white players have compared to their Black counterparts. Boosters and alumni are typically white, and they're more than happy to hire people that look like them, especially if they came from the team they love. Players who are persons of color aren't afforded these opportunities because we aren't members of the same 'club' that our white counterparts are beckoned into. Being a student athlete is valued on campus and off, but few experience the prestige it offers, especially when the color of their skin is seen first."

Players also pointed to the problem with the compensation they *did* receive in exchange for their labor: the cost of attendance scholarship and the degree that ultimately results – in other words, their education. In fact, the story itself is already told by graduation rates. While the graduation rate by 2019-2020 of the 2013-2014 cohort across Power Five schools was 78% for all undergraduates, that number fell to 68.6% for Black women's basketball players, 60.6% for Black men's football players, and all the way down to 46.7% for Black men's basketball players. These numbers offer a fuller measure of the exploitation of Black athletes on campus. In addition to being denied a fair portion of the revenue they produce through their labor, they also don't receive the full compensation they *are* promised: an education resulting in a degree.

Andrew described to us the feeling of being othered within academic spaces on campus: "I would purposefully not wear any team issued gear to class for the first few weeks in order to not be labeled as an athlete. Attending a PWI like I did brought enough negative assumptions about me without football adding to it. A decent number of my peers probably already thought I had gotten into the school because of my race instead of my merit, and professors weren't always exempt from this thinking."

Marla also picked up on this theme: "you know, I remember reading *The New Plantation* in a class and it makes a lot of sense to me. I often ask myself where I would be without basketball. Would I have had those opportunities? … Would I be accepted as a Black woman in the same way? Would I have been able to go to college? Would people on campus treat me the same? To be totally honest I think the answer is no way."

Just days after his claim that college sport is "modern day slavery," Geo Baker seemed to walk back his comment, clarifying: "I'm disappointed in the words that I used but I think there's a bigger discussion that needs to be made. The headline was three words that were at the very end of very truthful facts, that we are owned by someone else."

What Baker suggests is not so much that his analysis of college sports was incorrect, but that he is not permitted to name it for what it is. That too is a symptom of the white supremacist dynamics that shape and constrain the experiences of Black athletes in college sport today.

It's long past time for that to change. Power Five revenue sport *is* saturated in plantation dynamics that essentially amount to forms of unfreedom for Black workers laboring to earn revenue for white institutions and the predominantly white officials who govern them. The problem is not calling the conditions of college revenue sport racism, white supremacy, or a new plantation; the problem is that no matter what label we put on it, that is what it actually is, and it is exactly what a lot of very wealthy and powerful white people want it to be.

Print Citations

CMS: Kalman-Lamb, Nathan, Derek Silva, and Johanna Mellis. "'I Signed My Life Away to Rich White Guys': Athletes on the Racial Dynamics of College Sports." In *The Reference Shelf: College Sports,* edited by Micah L. Issitt, 105-110. Amenia, NY: Grey House Publishing, 2021.

MLA: Kalman-Lamb, Nathan, Derek Silva, and Johanna Mellis. "'I Signed My Life Away to Rich White Guys': Athletes on the Racial Dynamics of College Sports." *The Reference Shelf: College Sports,* edited by Micah L. Issitt, Grey House Publishing, 2021, pp. 105-110.

APA: Kalman-Lamb, N., Silva, D., & Mellis, J. (2021). "I signed my life away to rich white guys": Athletes on the racial dynamics of college sports. In Micah L. Issitt (Ed.), *The reference shelf: College sports* (pp. 105-110). Amenia, NY: Grey House Publishing.

Dangerous Stereotypes Stalk Black College Athletes

By Joseph Cooper
The Conversation, August 20, 2018

If you go strictly by the official account, heatstroke was the cause of death for University of Maryland football player Jordan McNair. McNair died earlier this year following a grueling practice in which training staff failed to properly diagnose and treat his condition.

But there's another culprit—or at least a contributing factor—that should not be overlooked.

As I argue in my forthcoming book—*From Exploitation Back to Empowerment: Black Male Holistic (Under) Development Through Sport and (Mis) Education*—what threatens black college athletes such as McNair is not just the brutal treatment to which they are subjected on the field.

Rather, it is a long-standing and deadly stereotype in American society that views black males as subhuman and superhuman all at once.

This stereotype, which is complex and has many layers, holds that black male athletes have superior athletic abilities that enable them to excel at high levels in sports such as football. The stereotype also holds that black males have a distinct physicality that allows them to endure extreme amounts of pain.

This is the same myth that was used to justify the enslavement and mistreatment of black people in America from before the Civil War through today's era of mass incarceration. In fact, a case can be made that there are many parallels between the exploitation of black student-athletes today and how black labor was exploited during American slavery.

McNair also appears to have fallen victim to a sports culture in the U.S. that promotes a win-at-all-costs mentality. This culture also places an inordinate amount of emphasis on generating revenue. And it represents a damaging view of masculinity.

I make these arguments as a scholar who focuses on the nexus between sport, education, race and culture.

Perceptions of Black Strength

I assert that black males in general, and black student-athletes in particular, are viewed primarily as physical beings–sometimes seen as "beasts" and the like. This dehumanizes them in ways that threaten their well-being.

Although such terms as "beasts" are widely embraced in mainstream culture and in some instances by black athletes themselves, such as Marshawn Lynch, whose "Beast Mode" clothing line is drawn from his nickname, these terms are still harmful. This is especially the case in sports, where masculinity is equated with toughness, playing through pain and not giving up.

It may be true that these ideas are applied to male athletes in general. But these views impact black males even more due to their unique experiences in the United States. Just as they did during the days of chattel slavery, I argue

> **It is a long-standing and deadly stereotype in American society that views black males as subhuman and superhuman all at once.**

that deeply embedded stereotypes about the physical capacity of black individuals to endure pain results in their perpetual mistreatment in the sports arena.

The stereotypes about black males' work ethic in sports like football and basketball has resulted in their higher incidences of cardiac deaths.

Not Valued for Intellect

Black student-athletes are also subject to educational neglect. Consider, for instance, the various academic scandals in big-time college sports. Some of these scandals involved cases in which black male athletes were found to be illiterate, but still allowed to compete in their respective sports and generate millions of dollars for the institutions.

Black males are often deemed as intellectually inferior and morally deficient. For example, black males are disproportionately more likely to be enrolled in special education courses versus gifted courses in the K-12 education system. They are also less likely than their white peers to have their race and gender associated with being intelligent or academic achievement.

For black male athletes, the dumb jock stereotype is commonplace and reinforced by the fact that they are more likely to be admitted to college academically underprepared, more likely to be enrolled in perceived "easy" or less rigorous courses so that they can remain eligible to play sports, and less likely to graduate compared to their peers.

Despite this academic neglect, black males continue to constitute a majority of the participants on football and men's basketball teams, 55 and 56 percent, respectively, in big-time college sports. This highlights how they are more valued for their athletic abilities than for their academic promise.

This is what enables sports organizers and coaches to present college sports to black males as a viable way to make it in society.

The view of black males as super-human is present in arenas other than sports. It lurks behind many of the police killings of black men of late. This was highlighted in the infamous police killing of Michael Brown in Ferguson, Missouri, in 2014, when police officer Darren Wilson described the 18-year-old Brown as a "demon" and "Hulk Hogan"-like.

Beyond the Glitz and Glamour

This type of pathological labeling applies in football. Black males' physicality is exploited. For example, at the University of Alabama, where head coach Nick Saban is paid US$11.1 million per year, black males represent 80 percent of the starters on the team. Yet, not only are black male student-athletes not equitably compensated based on market value for their athletic abilities, they also graduate at a lower rate—59 percent—compared to 71 percent for their athlete peers and 67 percent for the general student body. Thus, they are simultaneously academically underserved and athletically exploited in terms of economic compensation.

With both stereotypes—subhuman and superhuman—in play, black males within sport and beyond are systematically dehumanized and consequently deprived of the love, care and attention that should come with their humanity.

The large amounts of money being generated in college football, along with the increased commercialization and celebrity flair associated with the sport, creates an illusion of fun, American grit and a unique brand of entertainment.

But behind all the glitz and glamour are factors that contribute to the exploitation of athletes. These factors also result in undetected or undeserved—and entirely preventable—long-term health problems such as depression and high blood pressure, and in some instances, deaths.

The Need for Reform

In terms of medical coverage, colleges are not required to assist college athletes beyond their athletic eligibility years even though injuries they suffer in college can affect them for the rest of their lives.

Over the past several decades, organizations such as the National College Players' Association have advocated for increased medical coverage and protections for college athletes. The founder of the NCPA, former UCLA player Ramogi Huma, established the advocacy group after he discovered that the NCAA prevented UCLA from paying medical expenses from injuries that occurred during summer workouts.

University of Maryland President Wallace Loh recently stated that the university had accepted "legal and moral" responsibility in the death of Maryland football player Jordan McNair. That's a step in the right direction.

An acceptance of responsibility is not enough, though. Serious systemic reform and a change in culture is needed. These changes must address racism and racist stereotypes that lead to mistreatment of black athletes.

U.S. society must also confront its unhealthy obsession with sports glory, commercialism and overall neglect of athletes' rights and well-being.

One important reform that should be adopted immediately to benefit all college athletes is to require all medical staff for teams be independent from coaches' and athletic department authority. This was something reportedly proposed and rejected at the University of Maryland.

There should also be an advocacy group separate from the NCAA to help college athletes negotiate with the colleges they attend for improved working conditions related to safety and their overall well-being. This includes an improved academic experience, mental health support, and help with making the transition to their life after sports.

Print Citations

CMS: Cooper, Joseph. "Dangerous Stereotypes Stalk Black College Athletes." In *The Reference Shelf: College Sports,* edited by Micah L. Issitt, 111-114. Amenia, NY: Grey House Publishing, 2021.

MLA: Cooper, Joseph. "Dangerous Stereotypes Stalk Black College Athletes." *The Reference Shelf: College Sports,* edited by Micah L. Issitt, Grey House Publishing, 2021, pp. 111-114.

APA: Cooper, J. (2021). Dangerous stereotypes stalk black college athletes. In Micah L. Issitt (Ed.), *The reference shelf: College sports* (pp. 111-114). Amenia, NY: Grey House Publishing.

Gender Equality in College Sports Doesn't Have to Mean Separate

By David Webber
Columbia Missourian, April 9, 2021

Last week's NCAA men's and women's basketball tournaments heard allegations that women's facilities were not equal to those of men. The NCAA has hired a civil rights lawyer to investigate gender equity issues and to quell the controversy. In 2021, college sports appears to be overlooking a cliff of considerable change.

College sports got a wake-up call when California became the first of a dozen states to enact legislation requiring college athletes to be compensated for their institutions' use of an athlete's "name, image, and likeness." The NCAA is in the process of formulating specific provisions, but state legislatures are way ahead because of the interstate competition of college athletic conferences.

The Supreme Court is currently deciding a case based largely on the economics of the college sports industry and rights of individual college athletes to share in the revenues derived from their efforts. While athlete compensation is important, gender equity, long-term health concerns and promoting higher education values deserve more attention.

Sen. Cory Booker, D-New Jersey, is the major co-sponsor of the "College Athletes Bill of Rights" that includes enforceable health, safety and wellness standards, improved educational outcomes and opportunities and establishes a medical expense trust fund for individual athletes. However, the most attention-grabbing provision involves "fair and equitable competition," allowing athletes to profit from revenue related to the use of their "name, likeness, and image" and the sharing of tournament revenues that will benefit few athletes.

While public regulation of college sports is sometimes appropriate, the interests of higher education institutions, and the student athletes who attend them, would be better served if colleges and universities made a proactive effort to reimagine a whole new organizational regime for all college sports. To be credible, reform proposals must recognize the current funding macro-inequities caused by the oversized contribution of men's football and basketball. Bluntly put, the viewing and ticket-buying market for women's sports dwarfs that of men's sports.

Sports are the last American institution that stratifies participation based on gender. The rest of scholastic and collegiate education does not; the military does not; almost all occupations do not. Separating the recent NCAA women's and men's basketball tournaments raised concerns about the equitable treatment of women. So, combine the tournaments.

Boys and girls, men and women participate in sports together in many nonintercollegiate activities. In fact, we first learn about sports as boys and girls in youth T-ball or soccer leagues and in nongender-differentiated fun runs. Most competitive road races have men and women competing together but disaggregate the results according to age and gender divisions. Lots of men and women compete on equal footing in co-rec volleyball and softball teams in leagues across America.

At the highest level of college and professional sports, women are increasingly involved in men's sports as trainers, officials, team managers, coaches and high-profile sports announcers and journalists for men's baseball, basketball and football. There is no doubt that many women have developed the same sports acumen as men.

After more than four decades of court decisions and executive rulings, Title IX of the Education Amendments of 1972 requires that the number of athletic scholarships for men and women must be in proportion to the composition of an institution's student body. That usually means that at least 50% of scholarships be held for women

> **While athlete compensation is important, gender equity, long-term health concerns and promoting higher education values deserve more attention.**

athletes. That's fine until we consider men's football that has a huge roster—up to 125 players—and a large budget. If a college is required to award an equal number of men and women athletic scholarships, and if that college has a football program, simple math dictates that other men's sports need to be defunded. The resulting reduction in men's "minor" sports creates an inequity of its own, with male minor athletes ending up in extracurricular sport clubs.

Among the unintended outcomes of Title IX was one reported by CBS's *60 Minutes* that some universities eliminated men's minor sports, including men's gymnastics, in order to stay in compliance with Title IX. One national impact is that the university-based gymnastics network, from which many Olympic gold medals have come, is now down to only three universities offering men's gymnastics.

Three actions need to be taken to reduce college gender-differentiated sports while promoting gender equity that reflects broader societal values.

1. To the fullest extent possible, men's and women's competitions should be held at the same time and place. Furthermore, combined team scoring currently used in swimming, track and field and cross country should be expanded for sports such as volleyball, tennis and gymnastics. With a little imagination, combined team scoring in basketball, soccer and baseball/softball can be developed. With a little imagination, the NCAA championships, including basketball, could go to the university that has the best joint men's and women's rankings.

2. Sen. Booker's "College Athletes Bill of Rights" should modify Title IX's inter-pretation of proportional scholarships by providing institutional incentives for combined competitions and scoring.

3. That leaves the elephant in the room: college football. While first reactions are that football must remain exclusively a men's sport, it is possible to imagine that the grandeur, staging and revenue of college men's football can be shared with other sports, including women's sports. It is easier than you first think. First, the game day football field and venue can be shared with a soccer game or rugby contest. Secondly, the popularity and format of college football may change over time. There is currently an effort to form a college women's flag football league.

As the Supreme Court ruled regarding race and public education "separate means unequal." Reducing gender-differentiated college sports not only reduces gender discrimination, but it also prepares men and women to work and live together in a gender-equal society.

Print Citations

CMS: Webber, David. "Gender Equality in College Sports Doesn't Have to Mean Separate." In *The Reference Shelf: College Sports,* edited by Micah L. Issitt, 115-117. Amenia, NY: Grey House Publishing, 2021.

MLA: Webber, David. "Gender Equality in College Sports Doesn't Have to Mean Separate." *The Reference Shelf: College Sports,* edited by Micah L. Issitt, Grey House Publishing, 2021, pp. 115-117x.

APA: Webber, D. (2021). Gender equality in college sports doesn't have to mean separate. In Micah L. Issitt (Ed.), *The reference shelf: College sports* (pp. 115-117). Amenia, NY: Grey House Publishing.

NCAA Takes a Stand for Inclusion as States Target Trans Student-Athletes: Is It Enough?

By Dawn Ennis

Outsports, February 1, 2021

It's a new month, and more state legislatures are lining up to bar transgender girls from competing in girls' and women's sports.

As of today, Texas is the latest of at least 12 states taking aim at trans student-athletes, with more to come, specifically targeting college athletes.

Out athlete Chris Mosier has been one of the chief advocates leading the charge against these bills on social media.

As of yesterday, 12 states have anti-trans sports bills on the table, with Iowa & Mississippi closely mirroring Idaho's HB500, but with the difference of REQUIRING a genital inspection along with testosterone levels & a chromosome test. (Idaho's changed to one of the three ways)

— The Chris Mosier (@TheChrisMosier) January 30, 2021

At our request, the NCAA issued a statement clarifying its position on these transphobic bills, beginning with Montana's proposed legislation that would bar all trans student-athletes from competing except according to their gender assigned at birth. That bill passed the state House of Representatives on Jan. 27 and is now being considered by a state senate committee.

Outsports asked the athletic organization on Jan. 25 about the bill, HB 112. Here is the NCAA's response, received via email late Friday:

"The NCAA is aware of Montana's HB 112 and continues to closely monitor this bill, as well as other state bills and federal guidelines that impact transgender student-athlete participation.

"The NCAA believes in fair and respectful student-athlete participation at all levels of sport.

"The Association's transgender student-athlete participation policy and other diversity policies are designed to facilitate and support inclusion.

"The NCAA believes diversity and inclusion improve the learning environment and it encourages its member colleges and universities to support the well-being of all student-athletes."

This statement pales in comparison to the sharp rebuke the NCAA issued in 2016 when North Carolina enacted the so-called "bathroom bill," HB 2, which removed antidiscrimination protections for LGBTQ people, and banned trans people from using any bathrooms in public facilities that didn't match the sex they were presumed to be at birth.

Back then, the NCAA responded by moving the All-Star game and tournaments out of the state. Unfortunately, the association relented six months later, when N.C. lawmakers replaced HB 2 with a different bill. This one fell far short of a complete repeal, and at the time, our Cyd Zeigler called out the NCAA as "a fraud on LGBT inclusion."

Based on how the NCAA's latest statement was phrased, it may be time for another call-out.

Consider: In June 2020, the NCAA condemned Idaho's new law banning trans student-athletes, HB 500, calling it "harmful to transgender student-athletes and conflicts with the NCAA's core values of inclusivity, respect and the equitable treatment of all individuals." Advocates for trans inclusion called on the NCAA to move its college basketball tournament scheduled to be played in Boise in March 2021 out of state, and it was under consideration.

> **The NCAA must do more than just monitoring the situation . . . it must commit itself to the diversity and inclusion of college athletes by condemning legislation that would do harm to a portion of its athletes.**

More than 300 women athletes wrote to the NCAA last summer in support of the law, but did not sway anyone other than the usual transphobic lawmakers. Because of Covid-19, the NCAA wound-up moving all March Madness games to a single venue, and not in Idaho.

A federal judge put HB 500 on hold in August 2020, granting lawyers from the American Civil Liberties Union an injunction. That case remains unresolved.

Following an NCAA gender identity summit in November 2020, at which *Outsports* reported the stories of out transgender athletes had won over some hearts and minds, the NCAA governors repeated their strong stance against HB 500, stating: "the law is harmful to transgender student-athletes and is counter to the NCAA's core values of inclusivity, respect and equitable treatment of all individuals."

Compare those examples of firm support for trans student-athletes to this latest statement, promising to "closely monitor" HB 112, and there is a notable difference; a lack of teeth in the wording this time around. One former NCAA athlete offered his view:

"The NCAA must do more than just monitoring the situation. As the leading collegiate athletic association in the nation, the NCAA must commit itself to the diversity and inclusion of college athletes by condemning legislation that would do harm to a portion of its athletes," said rugby player, former NCAA wrestler and LG-BTQ trailblazer Justice Horn.

"As a cisgender athlete and the NCAA's first openly gay multicultural wrestler, I call on all LGBTQIA+ athletes and our straight allies to stand against this legislation of hate. I call on the NCAA to not only monitor the situation, but condemn Montana's HB 112. The NCAA should not be doing business, promoting, and holding NCAA championships with states who's elected leaders pass legislation that targets the many disenfranchised athletes who competes in the NCAA."

Print Citations

CMS: Ennis, Dawn. "NCAA Takes a Stand for Inclusion as States Target Trans Student-Athletes: Is It Enough?" In *The Reference Shelf: College Sports,* edited by Micah L. Issitt, 118-120. Amenia, NY: Grey House Publishing, 2021.

MLA: Ennis, Dawn. "NCAA Takes a Stand for Inclusion as States Target Trans Student-Athletes: Is It Enough?" *The Reference Shelf: College Sports,* edited by Micah L. Issitt, Grey House Publishing, 2021, pp. 118-120.

APA: Ennis, D. (2021). NCAA takes a stand for inclusion as states target trans student-athletes: Is it enough? In Micah L. Issitt (Ed.), *The reference shelf: College sports* (pp. 118-120). Amenia, NY: Grey House Publishing.

NCAA Warns State Lawmakers Against Limiting Transgender Sports Participation

By Chuck Lindell

Austin American-Statesman, April 12, 2021

In a statement supporting the inclusion of transgender athletes in sports, the NCAA Board of Governors warned state lawmakers Monday that actions to the contrary could result in the loss of championship games and events.

All student-athletes are expected to be treated with dignity and respect, the board said.

"Inclusion and fairness can coexist for all student-athletes, including transgender athletes, at all levels of sport," the Board of Governors said. "We are committed to ensuring that NCAA championships are open for all who earn the right to compete in them."

Texas is among 30 states weighing bills to ban transgender girls or women from participating in sports consistent with their gender identity, with governors in Mississippi, Arkansas and Tennessee signing such bills into law, according to the Human Rights Campaign, an LGBT rights organization tracking the legislation.

The Texas Senate could vote as early as this week on Senate Bill 29, which would block transgender athletes from participating in grade school and high school sports outside of their "biological sex."

SB 29 was designated as a priority by Lt. Gov. Dan Patrick, a Republican, and has 16 GOP senators as co-authors. After a Capitol hearing on SB 29 in which opponents, including many parents of transgender children, outnumbered supporters 4-to-1, the Senate State Affairs Committee advanced the bill on a party-line 5-2 vote with Republicans in favor and Democrats opposed.

The Texas House has taken no action on similar legislation, House Bill 4042, filed by Rep. Cole Hefner, R-Mount Pleasant.

Supporters of the transgender athlete bills argue that passage will protect competition and ensure fairness in girls sports, where they say transgender girls can have a physical advantage.

"Female athletes deserve their place in the record books for all of their hard work and dedication. We should not take that away from them," said Sen. Charles Perry, R-Lubbock, author of SB 29.

Opponents of SB 29 say it and similar efforts are an attack on the humanity of transgender people, further stigmatizing them while denying access to the benefits of sports participation, including camaraderie, sportsmanship, discipline, health, leadership and team building.

In its statement, the NCAA Board of Governors said it "firmly and

> **Supporters of the transgender athlete bills argue the passage will protect competition and ensure fairness in girls sports, where they say transgender girls can have a physical advantage.**

unequivocally" supports giving transgender student-athletes the opportunity to compete in college sports.

"The NCAA has a long-standing policy that provides a more inclusive path for transgender participation in college sports. Our approach—which requires testosterone suppression treatment for transgender women to compete in women's sports embraces the evolving science on this issue," the board said.

The NCAA requires that championships be held only where "hosts can commit to providing an environment that is safe, healthy and free of discrimination," the board said, adding that members will "closely monitor" the states to determine whether championships can be welcoming and respectful of all participants.

Championship events can bring a multimillion-dollar boost to a state and local economy.

Asked if Texas risked the loss of NCAA events if SB 29 were signed into law, board spokeswoman Michelle Brutlag Hosick said: "The most important thing to note right now is that the NCAA Board of Governors has not made a decision regarding championships and will continue to monitor the situation."

The board statement came less than two weeks after NCAA President Mark Emmert expressed similar concern over the transgender athlete bills, calling such legislation harmful to transgender students and contrary to the organization's core values of inclusivity, respect and equal treatment.

In Texas, Republican lawmakers also have filed several bills seeking to ban puberty blockers and gender-affirming medical treatment for transgender youths.

Two of those bills stirred strong passions during a Capitol hearing Monday, with supporters likening the treatment to child abuse while opponents, including transgender Texans and parents of transgender children, begged lawmakers to leave medical decisions to professionals and families who best know the issues in each case.

Print Citations

CMS: Lindell, Chuck. "NCAA Warns State Lawmakers Against Limiting Transgender Sports Participation." In *The Reference Shelf: College Sports,* edited by Micah L. Issitt, 121-122. Amenia, NY: Grey House Publishing, 2021.

MLA: Lindell, Chuck. "NCAA Warns State Lawmakers Against Limiting Transgender Sports Participation." *The Reference Shelf: College Sports,* edited by Micah L. Issitt, Grey House Publishing, 2021, pp. 121-122.

APA: Lindell, C. (2021). NCAA warns state lawmakers against limiting transgender sports participation. In Micah L. Issitt (Ed.), *The reference shelf: College sports* (pp. 121-122). Amenia, NY: Grey House Publishing.

Transgender Sports Debate Polarizes Women's Advocates

By Kathleen Megan
The CT Mirror, July 22, 2019

Before every race she enters, Selina Soule follows the same routine. She wakes up early and applies her signature meet make up—royal blue eyeliner to match her Glastonbury track uniform.

She struggles to choke down half of the egg sandwich her dad makes her, and then she listens to a "pump playlist" that includes the song "Win the Race" by Modern Talking to help get her into the zone.

"Just like my fellow competitors, I race to win," she said. "But that's virtually impossible now in an unlevel playing field."

Soule, a Glastonbury High School junior, believes the Connecticut Interscholastic Athletic Conference (CIAC) policy that allows transgender girls to compete in girls' sports without any hormone treatment is unfair.

That sense of injustice is at the heart of the complaint Soule and two other girls filed with the U.S. Department of Education's Office of Civil Rights in June arguing that their Title IX rights have been violated by a policy that they say pits girls against athletes who are biologically male despite their female gender identity. They contend the situation has robbed them of top finishes and possibly college scholarships.

With the CIAC policy in play, Andraya Yearwood of Cromwell and Terry Miller of Bloomfield—transgender girls who are track and field athletes—have grabbed national headlines and multiple championships, with Miller shattering state records in recent years and winning the Hartford Courant's girls' indoor track and field athlete of the year award in 2019. Both athletes also won the state's sportswriters' "courage award."

Experts in girls' sports and Title IX, the federal law that requires that women have equal access to sports, believe Soule and other cisgender athletes could have a valid complaint. They point out that both the NCAA and the Olympic Committee require transgender women to receive hormone treatment for at least a year and be tested for testosterone levels. The CIAC does not require either.

"I don't know of a woman athlete who doesn't want trans girls to be treated fairly," said Donna Lopiano, who led the Women's Sports Foundation for 15 years and now runs a Shelton-based consulting firm that works with clients on Title IX and other sports management issues. "But the cost of treating her fairly should not come at the cost of discriminating against a biologically-female-at birth woman."

Lopiano is hardly alone. The controversy over the inclusion of transgender athletes on girls' high school teams in Connecticut has deeply divided advocates who are usually in agreement when it comes to female sports, including lawyers, women's group leaders, athletes, and parents.

"It's amazing how polarized people get. Connecticut could be on the forefront of creating a structure or some way that lets both transgender and cisgender females fully participate, so that they both can be protected," said Felice Duffy, a former federal prosecutor with a law practice in New Haven that focuses on Title IX. "There's good people who will be very willing to talk about it and do it in way that makes sense."

It's a rift that has been driven even deeper by the involvement of the Alliance Defending Freedom, the group that filed the Title IX complaint on behalf of Soule and two other female athletes. The ADF has opposed allowing transgender girls in traditional girls-only spaces, including bathrooms and locker rooms.

But Doriane Coleman, a Duke University Law professor who has worked on the issue of sex in sport and has consulted with the National Scholastic Athletic Foundation, said ADF's participation shouldn't turn a non-partisan issue into a partisan one.

"This isn't bathrooms. Sports are different," Coleman said. "It's wrong to think of the OCR complaint as reflecting a right wing or conservative Christian position. It's not. People across the political spectrum care about ensuring that girls and women have an equal chance at the goods that flow from sport. The sports exception in Title IX, which allows schools to have separate teams for males and females, is about creating and protecting the space where this can happen."

For now, however, the sides are very far apart.

Recently, 16 Connecticut women's rights and gender justice groups—including NARAL Pro-Choice Connecticut, the New Haven Pride Center, and Planned Parenthood of Southern New England—signed a statement supporting "the full inclusion of transgender people in athletics."

"Transgender girls are girls and transgender women are women," the statement said. "They are not and should not be referred to as boys or men, biological or otherwise."

"We speak from expertise when we say that nondiscrimination protections for transgender people—including women and girls who are transgender—advance women's equality and well-being."

Changing the Definition of Gender

Title IX was passed 47 years ago to ensure an equal education for girls, but included a "carve out" allowing separate sports programs for girls because of the clear biological advantage that males have over females in athletics.

"It was the notion that there are distinct biological differences in sex that are immutable," Lopiano said, "namely after puberty, the effect of testosterone on males

… Everybody agreed that hey, if you have boys and girls competing after puberty, who would be more likely to get on a team? Who would win? It would be men. There would be very few women."

The current CIAC policy was developed in the context of federal and state law. A state law passed in 2011 prohibits discrimination based on sex or gender identity and does not require that a person's gender be determined by that individual's sex at birth, nor does it require a person to have undergone hormone therapy to be identified as a gender different from that assigned at birth.

The way Lopiano sees it, Connecticut's law says, "Hey, we are going to change the definition of sex," she said. "Now a woman is someone who identifies as woman, not someone who is biologically a woman… I'm not trying to criticize the definition, but that's in effect what the law is saying."

In a state that requires high schools to allow transgender girls to play sports with girls even if they have not had hormone therapy, Lopiano said, the challenge is how to do that fairly.

"I think you can do it, but not without an accommodation for their advantage," Lopiano said.

Duffy says she believes the way state law is being applied violates Title IX because it only disadvantages cisgender females.

"It's been shown that transgendered females who were assigned male at birth have the potential to be superior in power, speed and strength in sports, such as track, based on hormonal levels and other things," Duffy said. "And I would say to the converse, transgendered males assigned female at birth don't have the potential to be superior to males in track and field, for example. And therefore, there's no negative impact on cisgender males."

She said the NCAA and IOC rules further reflect this because they require transgender females to undergo hormone therapy to reduce their physical advantages.

"No one in Connecticut wants to discriminate against transgender girls, but by giving them the full go-ahead to participate you, in effect, are discriminating against cisgender girls from my perspective," Duffy said, adding that the inequity is particularly clear when it comes to post-season competition.

That was Selina Soule's experience.

Only a limited number of high school runners are allowed to advance to the state finals and Soule missed that chance in February when she came in eighth at the 2019 State Indoor Open in the preliminary 55-meter race. Only the top seven finishers were allowed to move on to the finals. Miller and Yearwood, the two transgender girls, occupied the two top slots.

"I respect these transgender athletes, and I understand that they are just following CIAC policy. But at the same time, it is demoralizing and frustrating for me and for other girls," Selina said in a recent email. "No matter how hard I try, I'll never be able to be competitive with someone who's biologically a male … No amount of practice and determination will ever get me or other girls to a place where we will have a fair chance to win. But the CIAC doesn't seem to care."

Her mother, Bianca Stanescu, said she has been surprised by the lack of support for her daughter and the other cisgender athletes.

"It's especially surprising and sad to see that most women's groups in Connecticut have lined up against fairness for girls," Stanescu said. "Why aren't they speaking up when girls are getting pushed to the sidelines and denied equal opportunities? Why aren't they seriously looking at the scientific and legal issues?"

Glen Lungarini, executive director of the CIAC, said that when he consulted with the U.S. Department of Civil Rights—months before the June complaint was filed — he was told that Title IX refers to sex but does not define what sex or gender is. "It reverts to your local legislature in terms of defining [sex and gender]," he said.

And he said, the state law is clear that a transgender girl should be treated as a girl. "They're not transgender, they are female," Lungarini said.

A statement from the CIAC said it will "cooperate fully if OCR decides to investigate this complaint. We take such matters seriously, and we believe that the current CIAC policy is appropriate under both Connecticut law and Title IX."

The policies on transgender high school athletes vary greatly across the country with some requiring birth certificates to prove their biological gender, while others require hormone therapy for transgender girls. Nineteen states and the District of Columbia have policies like Connecticut's that allow transgender athletes to compete in athletics with the gender they assert, without medical interventions, according to the Gay Lesbian & Straight Education Network.

> **For some advocates, however, allowing accommodations is tantamount to saying a transgender girl is not *really* a girl.**

"This isn't rocket science," Lopiano said. "I think there is a failure on the part of the CIAC to really think hard about how they can make a [fair sport structure] for both females at birth and those who self-identify as trans-girls, who choose not to alter their bodies. I don't have the answers but I know there are answers. There's not just one way to do this."

If a situation like the one that prevented Soule from going to postseason competition arises, extra slots for cisgender girls could be added, Lopiano said, to ensure that cisgender girls get to fully participate along with transgender girls. Or, she suggested, there could be classes for girls during post season competition as there are for wrestlers of different weights.

Coleman, the Duke University Law professor, said the Connecticut girls' Title IX complaint has finally brought a thorny issue to the fore.

"You wouldn't have called and asked me about this last year because it wasn't politically correct even to have the conversation," she said. "The cisgirls and their families and people who are aligned with their interests have really not had the space to speak because whenever they've tried, they've been attacked for being bad people. They are not bad people. They represent the traditional view of what Title IX is all about."

Coleman said she sees the complaint as viable particularly because the Trump administration has withdrawn the Obama administration's transgender friendly "guidance," and has made clear its preference for traditional definition—specifically that "sex means sex, it doesn't mean gender identity."

"It also happens that the majority of Americans, Democrats and Republicans, probably agree with them on this and that's dangerous for Democrats," she said. "I hope that liberal policymakers don't cede this issue to conservatives. You can believe, as I do, that equality for people who are transgender is important and that we need to find ways to make that a reality, while also acknowledging that it's a real leap to say that sex and gender identity are the same thing or that it's harmless to pretend that they are."

When Civil Rights Trump Fairness

For some advocates, however, allowing accommodations is tantamount to saying a transgender girl is not *really* a girl.

Kate Farrar, executive director of the Connecticut Women's Education and Legal Fund, said she doesn't see how a distinction can be made between the regular season and the post season "if we're working from a framework of equal access."

"The fundamental issues behind Title IX and a lot of our gender equity fights are in recognition of [the need for] equal access," Farrar added. "When we actually acknowledge transgender girls as girls according to their gender identity, we cannot deny them access. This is the whole point of why we have Title IX. Why we fought for gender equity."

"It really is a human rights issue at the heart of these opportunities for girls in our schools."

Dan Barrett, legal director of the ACLU of Connecticut, which has worked with the transgender girls, said the only question at issue in the complaint is whether Title IX permits the CIAC to adopt the policy it did.

"It's not whether there's a mandate to dream up something else," he said. Rather, he said it's whether the CIAC's policy is permissible under Title IX.

Asked about taking steps to accommodate cisgender girls, such as adding slots for cisgender girls in postseason competition or creating classes for women's sports, Barrett said, "that's not equal treatment and that's not going to fly in athletics."

Making such accommodations "seeks to get behind the person's gender identity," Barrett said, "and say whoever it may be, the athletic conference or school ... has decided that even though you're living your life as a woman and that's how you identify, we're going to mark you off as something different and place you somewhere else."

"In this case, it's pretty straightforward: These women were competing as women and that's the ballgame."

Barrett also compared the advantage transgender females have to the advantages that superior athletes of the same biological gender have in competition.

"I swam in high school. I was captain of the swim team ..." Barrett said, "but put me against Michael Phelps and it would not have been a contest. He was born with just an unbelievable wingspan."

Advantages in sports are not just limited to physical prowess or skill, he added, because some students have wealthy parents who pay for private coaching, strength training, or summer camps.

"No one is clamoring for a special league for those athletes," he said. "To do that to trans-athletes is not a particularly well disguised way of trying to discredit their choices, their autonomy as trans people."

High school coaches offer differing views of how the issue is playing out on the track.

Betty Remigino-Knapp, who coaches girls track and field at Hall High School in West Hartford and a former athletic director in the town, said her cisgender runners have sometimes felt demoralized after competing against transgender girls.

When one of her sprinters was "knocked out of the finals" by a transgender runner last year, Remigino-Knapp said, "she just walked away, pretty discouraged, wondering what the heck just happened."

"I have empathy for all kids ...but in regard to athletics, you know, we've always been given a fair and level playing field," said Remigino-Knapp, also a former track and cross country coach at UConn. "The physiological differences that males have over females — that's why we have female sports and male sports. Otherwise, we could really save the CIAC a lot of money and just have one coed championship."

Brian Calhoun, one of Yearwood's coaches at Cromwell High School, said there have been no conflicts since Yearwood joined the team, noting that one of Title IX's purposes, as he sees it, is to create athletic opportunities for a marginalized group.

"At first glance some people think the situation is unfair, but as you look at it, my overarching goals in athletics are to teach life skills and to help teenage athletes gather the skills that they'll need later on in life," he said. "If your goal is to teach our kids and prepare them for adulthood and you remember that's your goal, it really becomes a much more clear issue."

Both Terry Miller and Andraya Yearwood declined to comment for this story, but Rashaan Yearwood, Andraya's father, said he is not interested in "debating the biological features of men and women."

"This is only about my daughter being able to do what she wants to do. I don't really care about the athletic angle at all," Yearwood said. "Whether she wins or loses, she still would be running track. There have been plenty of cisgender girls who have beaten Andraya that have proven that Andraya being born male does not give her absolute dominance over the sport."

Robin McHaelen, executive director of True Colors, a non-profit group that advocates for LGBTQ youth, said that while she understands the issue of fairness raised by the cisgender girls, she ultimately sides with the transgender athletes, who "have already experienced so much oppression and hostility.

"The honest to God truth is I don't know what's fair, but I know that my role is to protect and care for the most marginalized of the kids we serve and I think that transgender girls, especially girls of color, fit that category," McHaelen said. "The reality is when you are talking about a civil rights issue, one person's discomfort does not override another person's civil rights."

Print Citations

CMS: Megan, Kathleen. "Transgender Sports Debate Polarizes Women's Advocates." In *The Reference Shelf: College Sports,* edited by Micah L. Issitt, 123-129. Amenia, NY: Grey House Publishing, 2021.

MLA: Megan, Kathleen. "Transgender Sports Debate Polarizes Women's Advocates." *The Reference Shelf: College Sports,* edited by Micah L. Issitt, Grey House Publishing, 2021, pp. 123-129.

APA: Megan, K. (2021). Transgender sports debate polarizes women's advocates. In Micah L. Issitt (Ed.), *The reference shelf: College sports* (pp. 123-129). Amenia, NY: Grey House Publishing.

The Fight for Transgender Athletes' Right to Compete

By Emilia Benton
Runner's World, March 18, 2021

In 2021, more NCAA athletes have had the opportunity to compete after shortened or canceled seasons because of the coronavirus pandemic last year. But for transgender athletes, a new challenge is confronting them across the country that could impede or outright stop their opportunity from participating in their desired sport. For transgender runners, one of the biggest hurdles they're facing is getting the general public and lawmakers to understand that they're not out there sweeping the podiums of all (or even most) of the races they're lining up for—they just want the chance to run.

In the latest challenge, Mississippi passed a new bill last week that bans transgender women and girls from competing in both youth and collegiate athletics. Idaho passed a bill in 2020, which was blocked by a federal judge, and South Dakota is nearing its own law. Similar laws in more than 20 other states are expected to follow after President Joe Biden signed an executive order in January extending protections against discrimination to gender identity and sexual orientation.

Many supporters of these bills say they want to protect opportunities for girls and women in sports, including things like access to scholarships at colleges and provide fairness to female competitors. "I will sign our bill to protect young girls from being forced to compete with biological males for athletic opportunities," tweeted Mississippi Gov. Tate Reeves on March 4.

In response to the string of new laws on the political agenda, more than 500 collegiate athletes from across the country sent a letter to the NCAA last Wednesday, demanding that championships and events be pulled in states that have passed or are considering passing laws that effectively ban transgender women and girls from participating in sports. (NCAA men's basketball tournament games were originally scheduled to be played at Boise State this year, but all games have been moved to Indianapolis because of the COVID-19 pandemic. South Dakota is set to host regionals or finals in several Division II sports and Division I men's ice hockey.)

In the letter to NCAA President Mark Emmert and the Board of Governors, signed by athletes from at least 85 schools across multiple sports, the athletes address the need for all to be provided safety and inclusion.

We, the undersigned NCAA student-athletes, are extremely frustrated and disappointed by the lack of action taken by the NCAA to recognize the dangers of hosting events in states that create a hostile environment for student-athletes. HB500 in Idaho, even with the current injunction, is still is an incredibly harmful bill that sets a dangerous precedent of subjecting all women athletes to potential invasive gender verification tests while also effectively banning transgender women athletes from competition. Multiple states are following suit this year and have already introduced bills similar to Idaho's HB500. You have been silent in the face of hateful legislation in states that are slated to host championships, even though those states are close to passing anti-transgender legislation.

To compete in sports, these bills often require an athlete to provide proof of their gender via a doctor's exam, genetic test, or hormone test to verify testosterone levels if an athlete's gender is called into question. These laws also, in effect, could overrule NCAA guidelines that do allow for transgender athletes to compete.

Lindsay Hecox, 20, is a sophomore at Boise State University who is part of the lawsuit challenging the Idaho bill and fighting for her right to compete on the school's cross-country team. While Hecox isn't allowed to participate with the team without being on it, per NCAA rules, the coaches have provided her a weekly training schedule to follow on her own. She occasionally runs with other students as part of an informal on-campus running club that isn't associated with any teams or intramural sports.

"These laws diminish trans women to being just men pretending to be women, and these lawmakers have no idea about trans vocabulary and what it actually means," Hecox told *Runner's World* in 2020. "Their argument is that trans women have the same ability as cisgender men, which is not accurate. I've lost so much athletic ability (in my transition) and no one really thinks about that or understands that."

Hecox noted that while it's been difficult to deal with lessened privacy and negative comments since going public with the lawsuit, it was important for her to become involved to bring attention to the harmful impacts such laws can have on athletes. According to *Sports Illustrated*, Hecox supports the recent letter to the NCAA.

"The average person doesn't really understand trans people—they should know that they have a very high rate of mental health issues just because of the fact that society has not really caught up and understood what it means to live a lie for a good portion of your life," Hecox told *Runner's World*. "I really hope that my fellow Boise State runners, if I do end up making the team, would not automatically assume I'm going to beat them."

What Are the NCAA Guidelines?

When the NCAA first released a set of policy standards for allowing transgender athletes to compete in 2011, the moment was groundbreaking for a minority group of runners who stood to be excluded without certain protections in place. Now, in 2021, runners and activists say the current policy is outdated and possibly contributing to controversy and discrimination that arises when transgender athletes see successes and wins.

The current NCAA policy on allowing transgender athletes to compete does not require gender confirming surgery or legal recognition of a player's transitioned sex in order for transgender players to participate on a team that matches their identity. However, it does require one year of hormone treatment testosterone suppression before as a condition prior to competing on a female team, though there is no such requirement for male transgender athletes to participate on a men's team. Athletes assigned female at birth are also still eligible to compete in women's sports unless or until that athlete begins a physical transition using testosterone.

In an email to *Runner's World*, a spokesperson for the NCAA said, "The NCAA believes in and is committed to diversity, inclusion, and gender equity for student-athletes, coaches and administrators. As such, the Association wants to maintain an inclusive culture that fosters equitable participation for all student-athletes."

"What we're seeing with the NCAA and the transgender athletes that are participating is they fit right in the range and the testosterone range of cisgender [gender identity matches their assigned sex at birth] female athletes," says Helen Carroll, an LGBTQ+ sports consultant who helped write the 2011 policy. "So they are playing in a very positive way with their teammates and coaches and opponents, and it's working quite well."

However, the NCAA doesn't monitor these athletes' testosterone levels in an effort to enforce the policy, which they would have to do with out-of-competition blood tests. This would serve to ease concerns about the need to prevent transgender athletes from having an unfair advantage against their competitors. This is a weakness of this rule, said Joanna Harper, a researcher and medical physicist who published the first study on hormone therapy in 2016. However, the study found that a nonelite group of eight transgender distance runners was no more competitive as women than as men, as transgender athletes faced lessened endurance, speed, strength, and oxygen-carrying capacity, showing that they didn't have a performance advantage over cisgender women.

With regard to the hormonal supplementation requirements, much of the general public may be surprised to learn that transgender athletes are not opposed to them. Many trans women will stay on hormone therapy for reasons unrelated to sports, but rather because they're happier and healthier that way, Harper says.

"Some may disagree and believe that they shouldn't have to undergo hormone suppression and suppressing their biochemistry just to be a part of something that they feel like they belong to," says CeCe Telfer, a transgender runner who competed at Division II Franklin Pierce University and won a national title in the 400-meter hurdles at the 2019 NCAA Championships. "However, I think that the NCAA has taken the most appropriate, accurate approach and steps into creating that common ground for everybody to be able to participate."

Chris Mosier, a six-time member of Team USA as a triathlete and duathlete, has also had a hand in reviewing the NCAA policy, as well as policies for national governing bodies, professional sports leagues, colleges and universities over the last few years. For NCAA athletes, Mosier feels it's time to evolve after a decade.

"When the original NCAA policy came out in 2011, it was one of the first and it really set the stage for inclusion and participation when there wasn't a lot of information available," Mosier says. "The policy has not evolved as our research and understanding and language has evolved, and it still currently includes terms like transsexualism and gender identity disorder, which are no longer applicable or relevant to creating a policy that works."

> **In 2021, runners and activists say the current [NCAA] policy is outdated and possibly contributing to controversy and discrimination that arises when transgender athletes see successes and wins.**

What Do Transgender Athletes Think?

According to Mosier, 40, by the NCAA estimates, less than 1 percent of the NCAA's student-athlete population is transgender, which isn't surprising, as only about 1 percent of the general United States population is transgender. This demonstrates that a decade after the NCAA enacted its current policy, not only are transgender women not dominating the sport, they are still vastly underrepresented.

"Hundreds of transgender athletes have participated in NCAA sports since the policy has been in place without a problem and without it being controversial," Mosier told *Runner's World*. "There aren't more transgender athletes now; there are just more people who feel comfortable enough and competent enough and safe enough to express who they truly are and continue to pursue their passions."

Telfer, 25, currently works as a licensed nursing assistant in Peterborough, New Hampshire, and is hoping to compete for the Tokyo Olympics in the 400-meter hurdles.

"These discriminatory attitudes hurt not only the transgender athletes who are participating but women's sports as a whole, because whether they're transgender or cisgender, women will always be questioned about their abilities, with people suspiciously saying they're too fast, too good, too strong," she says.

June Eastwood became the first transgender athlete to compete in Division I cross country while running competitively for the University of Montana as a senior before graduating last spring.

"It's understandable that (cisgender) athletes may be hesitant about competing against me because the science on it is so new and still developing and it's natural for people to want there to be as much competitive equity as possible," Eastwood says. "But I think that because we don't have the research right now, we should default to inclusion until we have more research and respond to the research as it comes up and ultimately create better guidelines so that the sport can be both as competitively equitable and inclusive as possible."

Eastwood, 23, also says that if the NCAA is seeking better inclusion, it needs to have a more diverse array of people when considering its new guidelines. Carroll added that the NCAA is currently working on updating the policy with language for nonbinary athletes and scientific research that's come out since it was first put forth.

Support from Their Sports, Not from the Community

"When I came out to my college community and track team, I was ready to come in with my lawyers and fight for the chance to compete as my authentic self," Telfer says. "I was pleasantly surprised to see that they were waiting for me to come out on my own terms and that they were ultimately very supportive of my journey to be the athlete I am today."

Even so, Telfer was aware that there would still be athletes and fans watching her compete who were outwardly opposed to her having the ability to be there. As a collegiate athlete, she grew accustomed to tuning the audience out.

"I just had that tunnel vision to just focus on what I was working so hard for, telling myself 'I'm here. I'm on the blocks, I'm on the line and it's time to execute,'" she says.

Eastwood shared that sentiment. She transitioned socially while still competing on the men's team before medically transitioning and running on the women's team for her final year of eligibility.

"Both teams were very supportive and understanding and it was as good an experience as I could have had, given the circumstances," she says.

However, she noted that she had a difficult time avoiding negative online commentary while competing in college.

"I've seen just about every negative thing that somebody could say about me and it's been hard to not let it affect me," she says. "It's even difficult now when people are still using me and commenting about me in these negative ways, and I'm no longer competing as a college athlete."

LGBTQ+ individuals often face unique challenges, including self-acceptance and acceptance by others, health and safety, and limited legal protections, which is why the NCAA operates its Office of Inclusion. The office serves to provide education and resources that support LGBTQ+ students and the coaches and administrators who teach and lead them in athletics departments across the country.

Mosier believes that while the NCAA has policies to allow transgender student-athletes to play sports, it doesn't necessarily have a system in place to fully support them when outsiders attack, whether it's in person or online. The new state laws are further fanning the flames and why he supports the NCAA athletes protesting these laws.

In 2016, the NCAA created an anti-discrimination statement and guidelines that would require host sites of NCAA events to meet certain qualifications— among them, host sites must "demonstrate how they will provide an environment that is safe, healthy, and free of discrimination, plus safeguards the dignity of everyone involved in the event."

Mosier thinks with its lack of clear and decisive action at this moment, the NCAA is not upholding the values it says it has.

"Banning athletes like me, forcing athletes to undergo invasive examinations, and telling people like me that we do not belong in sports is not a measure of fairness or respect," Mosier says.

That's why in 2013, Mosier founded transathlete.com, which serves as a resource to make sports more inclusive and to help athletes and their families, as well as coaches and athletic organizations, understand what the policies are in sport and the best ways to become involved.

Telfer said one area that non-transgender athletes and fans are largely unaware of is the added safety measures NCAA officials may take to protect these athletes at competitions, such as planning her travel, making sure her arrival and departure times did not coincide with those of other athletes, and having incognito security guards surrounding her. Telfer's coaches didn't inform her of these measures until after the fact to allow her to focus on the competition and avoid harassment.

"A lot of other athletes, i.e., cisgender athletes, don't always have to worry about being safe when they go out in public or at track meets," Telfer says. "In this regard, I believe the NCAA did a very good job of keeping certain situations under control and not letting them distract me while competing."

Eastwood is currently pursuing her master's degree in environmental philosophy at the University of Montana while also participating in local trail races with the goal of completing a 50-miler in the future. She hopes to eventually use her degree and experience to make outdoor communities more inclusive of LGBTQ+ people.

"My hope is that all people can go in open to the experiences of other people, not just in sports, but in all walks of life," Eastwood says. "I think that in meeting somebody like me or other trans athletes, this would help them realize that what they're reading that's targeted against us, isn't necessarily completely well-founded."

Print Citations

CMS: Benton, Emilia. "The Fight for Transgender Athletes' Right to Compete." In *The Reference Shelf: College Sports,* edited by Micah L. Issitt, 130-135. Amenia, NY: Grey House Publishing, 2021.

MLA: Benton, Emilia. "The Fight for Transgender Athletes' Right to Compete." *The Reference Shelf: College Sports,* edited by Micah L. Issitt, Grey House Publishing, 2021, pp. 130-135.

APA: Benton, E. (2021). The fight for transgender athletes' right to compete. In Micah L. Issitt (Ed.), *The reference shelf: College sports* (pp. 130-135). Amenia, NY: Grey House Publishing.

5
Professionals and Amateurs

Virginia Cavaliers and Duke Blue Devils by D. Myles Cullen, US Department of Defense, via Wikimedia.

The Supreme Court ruled in June 2021 against the NCAA's limits on education-related perks for college athletes.

The Pay-for-Play Debate

Collegiate athletics is a multibillion-dollar industry, and these massive revenues filter down through many levels of American society, enriching investors, shareholders, and individuals at many other levels. But what about the athletes whose effort and passion is the fuel for this economic behemoth? It is tradition that NCAA athletes, because of a philosophy known as "amateurism," do not and should not derive any direct remuneration for their participation in collegiate sports. But there are many critics who argue that this is unjust. With so many young women and men putting their health and welfare on the line as they work as hard as any professional in any field, some Americans believe that it is only fair for athletes to receive some portion of the revenues they help to generate. The debate over whether college athletes are entitled to compensation has been ongoing for decades, but broader cultural changes are adding urgency to this issue. One of these issues is the emergence of esports—virtual, digital competitions that are challenging traditional conceptions about athletics.

The Monetization of Sports

College sports has not always been a money-making machine. From the beginning of Western culture, in ancient Greece, athletic contests were very profitable for the state and provided one of the few ways that a person born into the lower levels of society might ascend to the elite. Even Grecians born into slavery could, if they succeeded as professional athletes, earn enough to place them in the aristocracy. This feature of professional sports has remained intact throughout the centuries, with many millions of young men and women born into poverty dedicating themselves to sport in the hopes of hitting the lottery in the form of a professional sports contract.[1]

While professional sports have always been lucrative, college sports began as something different. The first organized college sports in the United States were created as a way to refocus the inherent aggression and energy of young male students. Over the decades, sport became incorporated into the philosophy of American education. The idea was that young students needed to hone both their bodies and minds, and that organized athletic training and competition could provide long-lasting benefits. It wasn't long before collegiate sports became an important economic factor for colleges and universities. Colleges and universities learned that having sports franchises associated with their schools had many benefits, such as increasing interest from prospective students, helping to engage members of the public with the school, and creating a framework for long-term alumni and donor engagement. As institutions competed to field winning teams, more and more resources were devoted to this effort.[2] As college contests became more popular, colleges and universities began to see direct monetary benefits in terms of selling tickets and, much later, in terms of television contracts and the like. One of the figures most directly responsible for the monetization of college athletics is Walter Byers, the first NCAA division president and the man who organized the initial television deals that created the economic phenomenon of "March Madness."[3] Byers, the NCAA, and others helped build college athletics into a multibillion-dollar industry. But, as this occurred, the field became the target of criticism alleging that the focus on revenues intensifies the exploitation of student athletes.

Should Athletes Be Paid?

For decades, reformers have argued that it is wrong to maintain college athletes in a state of "amateurism" despite the industry's massive revenues and the effort and risks associated with being a college athlete. Less than 2 percent of NCAA athletes will receive a professional sports contract, and so only a vanishingly small number of college athletes will be in a position to earn serious money.[4] In addition, more than 90 percent of student athletes experience some kind of injury, and 12 percent suffer concussions or other potentially deadly injuries. Because the NCAA and colleges do not automatically provide medical coverage for student athletes, athletes are further risking their own financial well-being. The number of college athletes who suffer long-term medical issues as a result of their collegiate experiences is far higher than the percentage who can expect any serious financial remuneration.[5]

Given this risk and the seeming inequity of prohibiting college players from profiting from their efforts, many critics have argued that college athletes should simply be treated as professionals. The industry is certainly professional in terms of revenue, with many individuals enjoying lucrative careers by promoting college athletic contests. Some argue that athletes should enjoy a share in these revenues. This argument takes on another dimension when taking into account the large number of college athletes, especially athletes of color, who come from impoverished backgrounds. If the NCAA were to allow profit sharing, the revenues earned by athletes could transform their lives. It has likewise been argued that refusing to allow profit sharing means that the NCAA, educational institutions, and executives in the industry are actively profiting from the exploitation of minority and working-class athletes, while the financial benefits are enjoyed primarily by individuals in the upper classes.[6]

The arguments against paying collegiate athletes are complex, but typically revolve around the perception that it is important to preserve the relationship between education and athletics for the student-athletes who compete in collegiate leagues. Some argue that paying student athletes would essentially make collegiate athletics a job and so would discourage athletes from focusing on obtaining their education or preparing for a future career. Given that less than 2 percent of them will go on to have professional careers in sports, it can be argued that it is important for college athletes to engage in the educational aspect of their college experience. Other defenders of the current system argue that a system in which college athletes are paid might as well be considered another level of professional play rather than a part of the nation's collegiate system.

The tradition of treating college athletes as students rather than professionals has a long history in the NCAA. Walter Byers, the man who helped develop March Madness into a multibillion-dollar industry, was one of the people most responsible for maintaining this tradition. NCAA representatives like Byers have also argued that paying college athletes risks making participating in college athletics about profit, whereas many believe that participation in college athletics should be about the educational and personal benefits of the experience. Byers, a long-time champion of the view that collegiate athletics should remain an amateur field, eventually shifted position on the issue and argued that college athletes should be afforded salaries for participation. He was forced out of the NCAA when he changed positions on the issue.[7]

How Sport Is Changing

Broader cultural changes have brought this issue to the forefront of the public debate again. For one thing, a resurgence in the US civil rights movement has generated a public conversation about institutional racism and exploitation, and collegiate athletics has been cited as a racist and exploitative field in its treatment of minority athletes.

The spread of virtual and digital marketing has also opened up new revenue sources for college athletics and athletes, and this adds a new dimension to the debate over athletics and professionalism. With digital media providing avenues to bypass traditional streams of revenue, athletes have begun turning their athletic reputation into revenue for themselves. For instance, in January of 2021 a number of articles covered the story of Chloe V. Mitchell, a freshman volleyball player at Aquinas College in Michigan who developed a strong following on social media, with more than 48,600 followers on Instagram and 2.7 million followers on TikTok. Mitchell began gaining sponsors when she posted videos of her renovating a shed behind her house. As she has transitioned into college athletics, Mitchell has gained more and more followers, and she is believed to be the first college athlete to profit off of her likeness through sponsorships. Mitchell's success in marketing herself to companies eager to advertise on social media provides a loophole through which other college athletes could earn money from their popularity, if not directly from their participation in college sports. A number of other high-profile college players, like college basketball star Paige Bueckers, have also generated large-scale social media audiences that can bring in revenues without violating NCAA regulations about players being compensated for their performance.[8]

Another factor informing the debate over collegiate sports amateurism is the expansion of sports through digital media. The introduction of esports, or "electronic sports, is a controversy all its own within the world of college and professional athletics. Esports, which involves individuals playing video games in competitive contests, grew out of the informal tournaments that video game aficionados have been organizing for years. As these competitions started to draw more viewers and fans, corporations began to invest, setting up large-scale competitions in cities around the world. Through sponsorships and advertising, video game competitions evolved into a multibillion-dollar industry, generating huge amounts of revenues for video game and technology companies and the players themselves, who can earn revenues through sponsorships, paid streaming, and many other sources.[9]

In the 2010s, an increasing number of organizations officially began recognizing competitive video gaming as a "sport" and competitive players as "athletes." While it can be argued that competitive gaming requires both hand-eye coordination, strategy, and intelligence, some critics have taken issue with this activity being classed as a sport. Despite this, a number of higher learning institutions have seen the potential benefits of embracing this emerging industry. In 2019 Harrisburg University became the first to offer full scholarships to esports players, while a number of other institutions have used athletics funding to organize esports departments. Competitive video gaming draws in international audiences to a higher degree than traditional sports and is also more popular with younger spectators. With such a massive potential audience, esports revenues could soon rival the top draws in the world of big college gaming.[10]

Technology is redefining sports and how athletes can potentially benefit from their efforts and risks. Esports competitors are not restricted by age or by location, upending traditional barriers to participation. Just as esports players, ranging in age from elementary school to postcollege, can earn significant revenues through their own social media effort and sponsorships, athletes in traditional sports are also turning to technology and the social media marketplace to turn their own efforts into profit. This adds another dimension to the debate over college athlete compensation and signals that Americans may need to reconsider where to draw the line between professional and amateur in coming years.

Works Used

Branch, Taylor. "The Shame of College Sports." *The Atlantic*. Oct 2011. https://www.theatlantic.com/magazine/archive/2011/10/the-shame-of-college-sports/308643/. Accessed 25 May 2021.

Farmer, Angela. "Let's Get Real with College Athletes about Their Chances of Going Pro." *The Conversation*. Apr 24, 2019. https://theconversation.com/lets-get-real-with-college-athletes-about-their-chances-of-going-pro-110837. Accessed 26 May 2021.

Given, Karen. "Walter Byers: The Man Who Built the NCAA, Then Tried to Tear It Down." *WBUR*. Oct 13, 2017. https://www.wbur.org/onlyagame/2017/10/13/walter-byers-ncaa. Accessed 25 May 2021.

Hess, Abigail Johnson. "Meet Chloe V. Mitchell: One of the First College Athletes to Make Money from Her Likeness." *CNBC*. Jan 8, 2021. https://www.cnbc.com/2021/01/08/chloe-v-mitchell-the-first-college-athlete-to-monetize-her-likeness.html. Accessed 25 May 2021.

Smith, Ronald A. *Pay for Play: A History of Big-Time College Athletic Reform*. Urbana: University of Illinois Press, 2011.

Smith, Ronald A. *Sports and Freedom: The Rise of Big-Time College Athletics*. New York: Oxford UP, 1988.

"Student Athletes." *At Your Own Risk*. 2019. https://www.atyourownrisk.org/studentathletes/. Accessed 25 May 2021.

Willingham, A. J. "What Is eSports? A Look at an Explosive Billion-Dollar Industry." *CNN*. Aug 27, 2018. https://www.cnn.com/2018/08/27/us/esports-what-is-video-game-professional-league-madden-trnd/index.html. Accessed 25 May 2021.

Winkie, Luke. "Why College Are Betting Big on Video Games." *The Atlantic*. Nov 13, 2019. https://www.theatlantic.com/technology/archive/2019/11/harrisburg-university-esports-players-are-only-athletes/601840/. Accessed 25 May 2021.

Notes

1. Smith, *Sports and Freedom: The Rise of Big-Time College Athletics*.
2. Smith, *Pay for Play: A History of Big-Time College Athletic Reform*.
3. Given, "Walter Byers: The Man Who Built the NCAA, Then Tried to Tear It Down."
4. Farmer, "Let's Get Real with College Athletes about Their Chances of Going Pro."
5. "Student Athletes," *At Your Own Risk*.
6. Branch, "The Shame of College Sports."
7. Given, "Walter Byers: The Man Who Built the NCAA, Then Tried to Tear It Down."
8. Hess, "Meet Chloe V. Mitchell: One of the First College Athletes to Make Money from Her Likeness."
9. Willingham, "What Is eSports? A Look at an Explosive Billion-Dollar Industry."
10. Winkie, "Why Colleges Are Betting Big on Video Games."

NCAA Amateurism Appears Immune to COVID-19—Despite Tide in Public Support for Paying Athletes Having Turned

By Chris Knoester

The Conversation, November 30, 2020

Despite the coronavirus pandemic, college sports have mostly chugged along—albeit with cancellations, postponements and pauses in play.

While many college athletes are grateful for the opportunity to compete, the pandemic has laid bare just how few basic rights they possess. College athletes are navigating this strange sports season with increased health risks, but with little leverage or say about the conditions under which they'll play.

In contrast, their professional counterparts in leagues such as the NBA, WNBA, MLB and NFL, thanks to their respective unions, actively negotiated special accommodations, health measures, truncated seasons and the ability to opt out of playing. They also continually negotiate their economic rights, such as how their sport's revenue is split up and the minimum and maximum amounts that players may be paid.

Will this unusual season be the one that finally compels the NCAA to grant players broad economic rights, too?

The public, it seems, is increasingly on board.

According to a newly published study I conducted with Ohio University sports management professor Dave Ridpath, the tide in public opinion—at least when it comes to pay—has already been turning. However, race plays a big role in determining the level of support.

The Public Support Is There

In our study, we analyzed survey data that I collected from nearly 4,000 U.S. adults in late 2018 through early 2019. One of the questions we asked respondents was whether college athletes should be allowed to be paid, as athletes, beyond the costs to attend school.

Based on our findings, 51% of U.S. adults indicated support for this right by early 2019. This coincides with subsequent results from other polls that indicate rising levels of support for college athletes' basic economic rights. For example, an October 2019 Seton Hall Sports Poll found that 60% of U.S. adults supported college athletes being allowed to be paid for the use of their names, images and likenesses. Results from an AP-NORC survey in December 2019 pegged that support at 66%.

Previous research had consistently found that most U.S adults were opposed to college athletes being paid and were even against college athletes being able to negotiate for rights through a union.

The rising support for some basic economic rights for college athletes comes at a time when people are paying more attention to the massive financial hauls of some college sports programs, particularly through men's college football and basketball. These profits have led to enormous salaries for many coaches and administrators.

The NCAA has long claimed that college sports would lose their allure if college athletes were paid—that the magic of watching amateurs simply playing for pride while representing a cherished university would disappear, and fans would become less enchanted by college sports.

Yet we found that the most passionate sports fans were actually the most likely to support the idea of permitting college athletes to be paid.

Class, Race, and Amateurism

Race, however, does seem to influence respondents' support for college athletes' economic rights.

In our study, the odds for white adults strongly agreeing that college athletes should be allowed to be paid were 36% lower than those for nonwhite adults. When we zeroed in on Black and white respondents, we found that the odds for Black adults strongly agreeing with payment allowances were two-and-a-half times those of whites.

Why might this be the case?

It could have to do with the way race and class are intertwined with amateurism.

In the 19th century, white, upper-class Europeans invented the concept of amateurism. They claimed that paying athletes would corrupt the purity of the game and make participants more likely to cheat. In reality, they wanted to discourage working-class athletes from competing, as most couldn't afford to play for free.

When American universities adopted amateurism in the early 20th century as its model for college sports, these social class distinctions were still in play. There was also a racial element, since, at the time, higher education was the domain of the white and wealthy.

Over the course of the 20th century, nonwhite—particularly, Black—athletes were gradually integrated into college sports, which became increasingly commercialized. Today, Black athletes constitute an outsized proportion of college football and basketball rosters.

Yet amateurism, a relic of classist and racist attitudes, remains, and the bulk of the revenue that Black athletes disproportionately generate—a number that now amounts to billions of dollars—doesn't go to them. Nor have they or other athletes been permitted to accept outside payments aside from the full cost of attendance.

So, there is very much a racial element to the economic exploitation that seems to be occurring. But this is not solely a racial issue. Self-serving profit motives are also at play. The NCAA has inconsistently applied the principles of amateurism in order to exert more control over college sports and generate more revenue.

Still, perhaps the Black respondents in our survey were more aware of this discrepancy between profits, race and labor. We also discovered that—regardless of the respondent's racial identity—a recognition of racial discrimination in society coincided with greater support for college athletes' right to be

60% of U.S. adults supported college athletes being allowed to be paid for the use of their names, images, and likenesses.

allowed to be paid. This suggests that those inclined to perceive racial exploitation in American society might see college sports through the same lens.

Are the Times Finally Changing?

Pay, of course, is just one right. College athletes can be subjected to abuse, forced to risk their health and made to prioritize sports over academics—and still find themselves powerless to protest or enact changes.

Thanks to athlete activism, media attention, legal challenges, state legislation and shifts in public opinion on the issue of economic rights, the NCAA seems to be on the precipice of allowing college athletes to receive some forms of additional compensation.

In April, after being pressed to allow college athletes to profit from the use of their names, images and likenesses, the NCAA signaled that they will grant permission for this and will vote on proposals in January 2021. A Florida law is slated to permit this to occur in their state with or without NCAA approval in the summer of 2021.

If the NCAA won't grant basic economic and other rights to college athletes, it might be up to lawmakers to keep applying the pressure. That's exactly what a group of senators tried to do in August when they introduced a College Athletes Bill of Rights that would guarantee NCAA players financial compensation, representation, long-term health care and lifetime educational opportunities.

The bill is languishing in the Senate, where it currently lacks any Republican support. Until that changes, it may be up to the athletes themselves to raise awareness and instigate change.

Print Citations

CMS: Knoester, Chris. "NCAA Amateurism Appears Immune to COVID-19—Despite Tide in Public Support for Paying Athletes Having Turned." In *The Reference Shelf: College Sports,* edited by Micah L. Issitt, 145-148. Amenia, NY: Grey House Publishing, 2021.

MLA: Knoester, Chris. "NCAA Amateurism Appears Immune to COVID-19—Despite Tide in Public Support for Paying Athletes Having Turned." *The Reference Shelf: College Sports,* edited by Micah L. Issitt, House Publishing, 2021, pp. 145-148.

APA: Knoester, C. (2021). NCAA amateurism appears immune to COVID-19—despite tide in public support for paying athletes having turned. In Micah L. Issitt (Ed.), *The reference shelf: College sports* (pp. 145-148). Amenia, NY: House Publishing.

The Man Responsible for Making March Madness the Moneymaking Bonanza It Is Today

By Rick Eckstein
The Conversation, March 14, 2018

In a legendary *South Park* episode lampooning the NCAA, the character Eric Cartman asks a university president if he can purchase some of his "slaves" —er, "student-athletes" —who play men's basketball.

"How do you get around not paying your slaves?" Cartman wonders.

The outraged university president kicks Cartman out of his office. But if the president were being honest, all he would have to do is utter one name: Walter Byers.

Byers served as the NCAA's first executive director from 1951 to 1988. During this period, the NCAA evolved from an insignificant advocate of athletic integrity into an economic powerhouse.

One critical piece of this growth was the creation of a narrative about the amateur purity of college sports. Walter Byers, who made "student-athlete" part of the American lexicon, played a central role in this enterprise. The NCAA, meanwhile, would become increasingly reliant on March Madness to finance its operations.

Cashing in on March Madness

Contrary to popular belief, college football provides the NCAA with almost no revenue.

A landmark 1985 U.S. Supreme Court decision found that TV revenues for college sports would go to the various athletic conferences rather than to the NCAA. The NCAA still "regulates" college football. It just doesn't get a piece of the pie.

The same is true for regular season and conference tournament college basketball games. Only March Madness makes money for the NCAA since it is run by the NCAA and schools are "invited" to play in it. Indeed, for many years schools often chose to play in the more prestigious National Invitation Tournament, which, since it was held in New York City, received much more of the media attention that colleges craved.

By the end of the 1960s, though, the NCAA tournament started to become more appealing to colleges than the National Invitation Tournament. Under Byers' quiet direction, the NCAA in-vited a larger number of teams to its tournament and paid all of their ex-penses. This subsidy was made possible by the

---

March Madness generates roughly US$900 million per year, good for over 80 percent of the NCAA's total annual revenue.

---

organization's then-significant broadcasting revenue from college football (which would subsequently end in 1985). The National Invitation Tournament couldn't compete with this business model and eventually faded to second-class status.

Just how important is March Madness to the NCAA's current financial health?

The annual tournament generates roughly US$900 million per year, good for over 80 percent of the NCAA's total annual revenue. The NCAA uses the bulk of its income to run the organization, give payments to conferences and subsidize nonrev-enue sports championships. Even so, the NCAA accumulated a surplus in 2014 of $81 million. Tournament revenue is slated to reach $1.1 billion per year after 2025.

It wasn't always that way. In the 1970s, the tournament itself probably cost more than it made, although there is only scant anecdotal data on this. In 1982, the tour-nament generated about $17 million per year. Thus, tournament revenues increased 5,200 percent over 35 years, significantly outpacing inflation over that same period.

Expanded competition for broadcasting rights, fueled by the birth of cable chan-nels like ESPN, turned this once sleepy tournament into the NCAA's organizational cash cow.

The "Student-Athlete" Is Born

But this moneymaker might not have developed at all if Walter Byers hadn't coined the term "student-athlete" in the mid-1950s.

The term emerged as the NCAA defended itself in a worker's compensation claim by the widow of Ray Dennison, who had died in 1954 while playing football for Fort Lewis A&M in Colorado. His widow likened college football to a full-time job, and argued that his death should be covered by state labor laws.

Byers and the NCAA's lawyers countered that Dennison was a "student-athlete" participating in an extracurricular activity that just happened to be more dangerous than, say, singing in the glee club. The courts agreed with the NCAA.

Since then, Byers' "student-athlete" moniker has become the semantic center-piece for the NCAA's claim that college sports is inherently noncommercial. You'll rarely hear anyone in the college sports industry not use the term "student-athlete" when referring to varsity players.

Regrets, He Had a Few

Whether or not there really is such a thing as a "student-athlete," the idea behind the phrase has served the NCAA well for over 60 years.

It allows the NCAA to advertise college basketball as a fundamentally different product than professional basketball—and a better product at that. They can say that March Madness isn't filled by professional athletes and team owners only interested in making a buck. Rather, the participants are student-athletes who simply love playing the game.

Throughout the tournament, the NCAA will regularly tout the fact that 97 percent of student-athletes won't become professional athletes. Video vignettes air during commercial breaks and on jumbotrons reminding fans that these players ask questions in class and will one day put away their uniforms and sports equipment in favor of lab coats and briefcases.

But the student-athlete moniker isn't just about selling a product. It's about maximizing the revenue from these products. By claiming that college sports is educational rather than commercial, the NCAA can maintain its IRS 501(c)(3) tax-free status. If subjected to federal and state taxes, the $880 million of March Madness revenue could be reduced by 40 percent or more. (The NCAA also doesn't pay property taxes on its palatial headquarters in Indianapolis.)

One of the great ironies in all this is that Walter Byers eventually learned to loathe the college sports behemoth he helped create.

In his 1997 autobiography, Byers lamented that modern college sports were no longer a student activity—that they had instead become a high-dollar commercial enterprise. He argued that athletes should have the same rights as coaches and be able to sell their skills to the highest bidder.

In short, he came to agree with Cartman: The term "student-athlete" is merely a euphemism used to ensure schools and the NCAA can maximize their profits.

Print Citations

CMS: Eckstein, Rick. "The Man Responsible for Making March Madness the Moneymaking Bonanza It Is Today." In *The Reference Shelf: College Sports,* edited by Micah L. Issitt, 149-151. Amenia, NY: Grey House Publishing, 2021.

MLA: Eckstein, Rick. "The Man Responsible for Making March Madness the Moneymaking Bonanza It Is Today." *The Reference Shelf: College Sports,* edited by Micah L. Issitt, Grey House Publishing, 2021, pp. 149-151.

APA: Eckstein, R. (2021). The man responsible for making March Madness the moneymaking bonanza it is today. In Micah L. Issitt (Ed.), *The reference shelf: College sports* (pp. 149-151). Amenia, NY: Grey House Publishing.

How College Sports Turned into a Corrupt Mega-Business

By George Leef

James G. Martin Center for Academic Renewal, March 11, 2020

College sports are a gigantic entertainment business that have nothing to do with the missions of the schools. Frequently, the highest-paid employee of a school is the football or basketball coach, and the athletics budget is hugely subsidized by fees paid by financially strapped students. Players who read and write at a middle-school level (if even that) are recruited to help teams win, but the academic work they do is laughable. Schools rack up big debts trying to win glory on the gridiron or court, even if it means scrimping on faculty salaries and building maintenance.

How did this lamentable state of affairs come about?

To find out, the book to read is *Intercollegiate Athletics, Inc.* by professor James T. Bennett. He has researched the history of college sports in America, starting with the earliest days (when contests were organized and run by students for their own enjoyment) up to the latest scandals and perversions. He explains how the sports juggernaut gathered force (first football, later basketball) and recounts the various efforts (mostly unsuccessful) to stop or at least slow it. And perhaps most usefully, he points out that the high cost of college sports falls mainly on students through mandatory fees—a tax on education that goes to benefit a pampered few.

If you're bothered by the fact that, as the author reports on a recent study, Division I schools (the top level in the NCAA's hierarchy) spend three to six times as much on athletics per athlete as they do on academics per student, then this is a book you'll want to read.

The first intercollegiate sporting competition was not football, but rowing, when the Harvard and Yale teams met in 1852. Football started to gain popularity in the 1870s when students began organizing games between rival colleges. By the turn of the century, football was *big*. Winning had become so important that teams routinely brought in "ringers," which is to say, good players who weren't students at all. Injuries were common.

The first college presidents to speak out against this spectacle were Charles Eliot of Harvard and Nicholas Murray Butler of Columbia. Eliot criticized the "immoderate desire to win" that led to cheating and the militaristic aura surrounding football. At Columbia, Butler decided to abolish football in 1905, calling it an "academic nuisance" that interfered with studying. Butler's abolition lasted only a decade, however.

From the Northeast, football soon spread to the South and the Midwest, where the problems identified by Eliot and Butler grew apace. One academic leader who tried to tame football's malign influence was UNC president Frank Porter Graham. In 1935, he drew up a proposal to ban the recruitment of players and any preferential treatment of athletes in the awarding of scholarships, jobs, or loans.

How well was Graham's proposal received? Bennett quotes him as saying that his critics "opened up with machine guns, and in some cases poison gas." Attacked by alumni and many of the politicians who voted for UNC appropriations, Graham backed down quietly. Although he served until 1949, he never again attempted to do anything about the growing tumor of college football.

The high costs of college sports falls mainly on students through mandatory fees—a tax on education that goes to benefit a pampered few.

In the Midwest, the University of Chicago was king of the football realm in the 1920s and 1930s. The university's president, William Rainey Harper, hired the famous coach Amos Alonzo Stagg and gave him *carte blanche* to win. Stagg did exactly that. His methods were often unscrupulous, but the "Monsters of the Midway" became a powerhouse. But when Robert Maynard Hutchins was named president in1929, he was extremely unhappy with the situation. He thought that sports should be merely an ancillary function of a university. "A college racing stable makes as much sense as college football," he said.

Under Hutchins, Chicago instituted a rule that football players had to take the same courses as all other students, and that pulled the rug out from under Stagg's mighty team. By 1939, it was a doormat, losing by such scores as 61-0 to Harvard and 85-0 to Michigan. At the end of that season, Hutchins announced that Chicago would drop intercollegiate football.

In a speech to the students, he explained his reasons: "I hope that it is not necessary for me to tell you that this is an educational institution, that education is primarily concerned with the training of the mind, and that athletics and social life, though they may contribute to it, are not the heart of it and cannot be permitted to interfere with it."

To the saga of Chicago football, Bennett adds this humorous ending: "The Maroons locker room would be converted to house the Manhattan Project, giving a new meaning to the phrase *long bomb.*"

We learn that several other universities have also dropped football, including the University of Seattle and the University of Denver. Getting out of that costly extravaganza is feasible, although a university president who proposes it must be ready for fierce opposition.

Consider the tale of Ray Watts, president of the University of Alabama at Birmingham (UAB). Football is almost a state religion in Alabama, but UAB wasn't very successful and program costs were heavily subsidized by student fees and the university's general budget. In 2014, looking at a bleak financial picture, Watts decided that the money football was absorbing would be better spent on academics and announced that the university was dropping the sport.

Poor President Watts—he hadn't counted on the ferocious opposition to his pro-academic priorities. He was roasted in the press, excoriated by the alumni, and even the faculty lashed out with a vote of no confidence. To save his hide, Watts reversed field. After a fundraising drive brought in $20 million, he announced that football would be back in 2017. It is back, and so are the high costs.

On the other hand, if a college president wants to add big-time sports or move up to a "higher" conference, he'll find plenty of support. He can hire consulting firms to produce "research" that will demonstrate how a sports move will have great long-term benefits. In such studies, the costs are always downplayed while the supposed benefits (such as increased school loyalty) are hyped.

This has "worked" at a number of schools, including UNC-Charlotte. In 2007, chancellor Philip Dubois decided that his school's reputation would soar if it started playing top-level football. He got his way. Millions were spent to build the necessary stadium and hire the coaches. Student fees went from an already lofty $1,160 per student to $1,648. Since starting play in the Sunbelt Conference in 2008, UNCC teams haven't won many games, but even if they had, is there any reason to believe that the institution would be the least bit better? Bennett doesn't think so.

But sometimes common sense prevails and the idea of boosting school prestige through sports is shot down. One such case was at another UNC institution, Winston-Salem State. The administration foolishly committed to moving up to NCAA Division I in 2007. But three years into its transition, a new chancellor concluded that the cost, which included $10 million in facility upgrades, was not justified and the school went back to competing in Division II. No sense in throwing good money after bad.

Bennett's penultimate chapter explores the way women's sports have followed the ruinous path of men's athletics, beginning in the 1970s. That topic merits a separate article.

And that brings us to the ultimate chapter: "Reform—or Renewal?"

Bennett is not optimistic that college sports will change for the better. Few college presidents have the backbone for a fight with the entrenched athletics establishment, the faculty is generally not interested in battling it, and hardly any students care much about the cost that athletics adds to their bills. How about federal intervention? Bennett mentions some legislative ideas that have been floating around Congress but isn't enthusiastic about any.

How about paying college athletes? Bennett gives that idea the back of his hand. He writes, "If college football and basketball players do join the ranks of the officially salaried, we will have the strange spectacle of ordinary students paying increased fees in order to subsidize not just the education but the livelihoods, the salaries, of their far more feted and celebrated sports-playing fellow 'students.' And if you pay those who play revenue sports, the big-time sports factories may need to shutter nonrevenue sports, which would run afoul of Title IX."

If you read *Intercollegiate Athletics, Inc.* you'll be convinced that we have a serious problem, but also that it's a problem with no evident solution.

Print Citations

CMS: Leef, George. "How College Sports Turned into a Corrupt Mega-Business." In *The Reference Shelf: College Sports,* edited by Micah L. Issitt, 152-155. Amenia, NY: Grey House Publishing, 2021.

MLA: Leef, George. "How College Sports Turned into a Corrupt Mega-Business." *The Reference Shelf: College Sports,* edited by Micah L. Issitt, Grey House Publishing, 2021, pp. 152-155.

APA: Leef, G. (2021). How college sports turned into a corrupt mega-business. In Micah L. Issitt (Ed.), *The reference shelf: College sports* (pp. 152-155). Amenia, NY: Grey House Publishing.

Paying College Athletes

By Brianna Rauenzahn, Jamison Chung, and Aaron Kaufman
The Regulatory Review, February 6, 2021

College student athletes generate millions of dollars in profits for schools, coaches, and conference and network executives—everyone, it seems, but themselves.

College athletics operate under the National Collegiate Athletic Association (NCAA), a private nonprofit organization. Under current NCAA regulations, compensation for student athletes is limited to scholarships for their education. Meanwhile, universities enter multimillion dollar deals with cable networks and athletic brands—all of which profit from using athletes' images in marketing campaigns, apparel sales, and ticket sales, among other revenue.

In 2019, the California legislature passed a law in direct opposition to these NCAA regulations. California Governor Gavin Newsom noted that currently every college student, except athletes, can use social media and other platforms to market and monetize their name, image, and likeness.

This restriction on college athletes will change under the new Fair Pay to Play Act, set to take effect in 2023. California student athletes will be able to monetize their social media followings, provide paid coaching, enter endorsement and advertising deals, and hire agents. Although the law allows student athletes to profit from third-party deals, it does not require, or even allow, schools to pay student athletes for their work beyond the scholarships they already receive.

After some NCAA officials expressed concern that the Fair Pay to Play Act will advantage California schools in recruiting top athletes, the organization is working to change its long-standing athlete pay regulations. The NCAA board of governors recommended that its three divisions adopt new rules that would allow student athletes to receive compensation from the use of their name, image, and likeness. The NCAA expects this unprecedented rule change to apply for the 2021 to 2022 school year.

In addition, a federal court recently found that NCAA limitations on student athlete compensation violate antitrust law. The NCAA, the court held, could preserve amateurism in college sports while increasing the organization's current caps on education-related benefits that athletes can receive. The U.S. Supreme Court will soon review that decision, which paves the way for athletes to receive greater benefits such as "graduate school scholarships, study abroad opportunities, or computers."

Some commentators worry that pay-to-play rules would diminish the spirit of amateurism in college athletics. Others argue that the current system exploits student athletes—especially Black athletes who dominate the two biggest revenue-generating college sports, football and basketball. Some experts also note that new pay-to-play rules could benefit female college athletes who often have fewer opportunities than men to profit from their sport after college.

This week's Saturday Seminar explores legal issues surrounding pay-to-play rules and the future of amateurism in college sports.

- In an article in the *Harvard Journal of Sports and Entertainment Law*, Indiana University's Jayma Meyer and Smith College's Andrew Zimbalist propose a federal framework to pay student athletes for use of their name, image, and likeness. Under this framework, universities could profit from using this information for limited purposes, such as promoting athletic events and selling official team apparel. Athletes could then enter into endorsement deals with third parties if the agreement does not conflict with the schools' right to use their images. Meyer and Zimbalist urge the U.S. Congress to establish an independent commission to regulate these payments. They recommend that the commission pass regulations—such as maximum income and academic standards—to ensure that student athletes' academic success remains a priority over their athletic success.

- James Landry of the De Novo Agency and Thomas A. Baker III of the University of Georgia also propose a new model for payments to college athletes for their name, image, and likeness. In an article in the *NYU Journal of Intellectual Property and Entertainment Law*, they conclude that "no reason in law or common sense" justifies the current NCAA ban on these payments. If the NCAA changes its athlete compensation rules and permits athletes to hire agents, Landry and Baker recommend that the organization also create an "agency certification process" to protect athletes from untrustworthy sports agents. Landry and Baker also suggest adopting academic eligibility criteria as a condition of payments, which would prevent both athletes and universities from profiting if athletes' grades fall below a certain level.

- In a recent article, Kevin D. Brown and Antonio Williams of Indiana University examine the ramifications of the amateurism model—limiting athlete compensation to the cost of attending school—on major revenue-generating college sports such as Division I football and Division I men's basketball. Because Black students are over-represented in high revenue-generating sports, Brown and Williams worry about the potential for racial exploitation in applying the amateur model. They acknowledge that substantial legal obstacles deter abandoning amateurism, such as the effect of athlete pay on universities' federal income taxes. Instead of abandoning amateurism altogether, Brown and Williams recommend reallocating some of the revenue from college sports to fund programs to increase higher education outcomes for all members of the Black community.

- In a forthcoming article in the *West Virginia Law Review*, Sam C. Ehrlich of Boise State University examines the employment law implications of lifting the NCAA ban on paying student athletes. Operating under the assumption that student athletes will become statutory employees of their colleges under the Fair Labor Standards Act (FLSA), Ehrlich considers whether athletes' current compensation—tuition, housing, and food—can be credited toward minimum wages. To count toward minimum wages under the act, employers must provide regular benefits that primarily aid the employee, who must then voluntarily accept the benefits. Ehrlich argues that, although food and housing could count toward minimum wage, college tuition is not creditable under FLSA.

  > **This restriction on college athletes will change under the new Fair Pay to Play Act, set to take effect in 2021.**

- Roberto L. Corrada of the University of Denver Sturm College of Law argues in a *Chicago-Kent Law Review* article that certain institutions of higher education will soon consider student athletes employees of their respective institutions. Corrada suggests tweaking S. Department of Labor regulations to reclassify student athletes under a category similar to a work-study program. Accommodating student athletes under a system modeled after the Federal Work-Study Program could make them eligible for other benefits such as "sick leave, paid-time off, health care, and workers compensation," but could also "trigger a host of other employment-related obligations," including unemployment insurance, Corrada explains.

- Marc Edelman of the Zicklin School of Business at Baruch College argues in a *Wake Forest Journal of Business and Intellectual Property Law* article that the NCAA violates Section One of the Sherman Antitrust Act when it threatens to ban universities that permit student athlete endorsement deals. Edelman contends that the NCAA banning its members would be anticompetitive economically and harmful to consumers of college sports. Without competition among recruiting schools, college sports fans cannot express their preference for certain athletes. Because no federal statutes or common law policies "preempt the application of antitrust law" in this situation, the NCAA's possible arguments to defend against antitrust charges would be weak, Edelman argues.

Print Citations

CMS: Rauenzahn, Brianna, Jamison Chung, and Aaron Kaufman. "Paying College Athletes." In *The Reference Shelf: College Sports,* edited by Micah L. Issitt, 156-159. Amenia, NY: Grey House Publishing, 2021.

MLA: Rauenzahn, Brianna, Jamison Chung, and Aaron Kaufman. "Paying College Athletes." *The Reference Shelf: College Sports,* edited by Micah L. Issitt, Grey House Publishing, 2021, pp. 156-159.

APA: Rauenzahn, B., Chung, J., & Kaufman, A. (2021). Paying college athletes. In Micah L. Issitt (Ed.), *The reference shelf: College sports* (pp. 156-159). Amenia, NY: Grey House Publishing.

Paying College Football Players Is Only Fair

By Stephen L. Carter
Bloomberg, November 7, 2020

A professor at Ohio State recently joined the apology parade so tragically common these days in academia. His offense was having expressed a positive view of college football. In his abject state of remorse, he confessed to having given insufficient attention to how the export exploits young Black men.

Although coerced apologies are inimical to academic freedom, there's a good case to be made that colleges are indeed guilty of exploiting their football players, about half of whom are Black. As so often, the solution is a free market: To avoid exploitation, pay the players their market value.

Right now, the big-time football schools (known as the "Power 5") essentially run a cartel, under the management of the National Collegiate Athletic Association. The cartel limits the pay and benefits players can receive in return for their services. As the economists Allen R. Sanderson and John J. Siegfried note in a 2015 article in the *Journal of Economic Perspectives*, college athletics is the only part of campus life in which an outside entity is allowed to limit wages. Thus, the substantial rents provided by Power 5 football are retained by the schools.

And even putting aside the television and ticket revenue big-time football brings in, the gains from fielding competitive football teams are considerable. Sanderson and Siegfried point to prior research showing that state legislatures appropriate significantly more money to schools that field football teams than to similarly situated schools that don't. More recent work finds that within the big football conferences, success on the field predicts higher alumni giving to athletics (for giving outside athletics, the data are unclear), more and better applications for admission, and an increase in a school's overall academic reputation—all made possible by the cartel.

Like many football fans, I worry that the players this system exploits are disproportionately Black. 1 An August 2020 working paper from the National Bureau of Economic Studies confirms this instinct. By analyzing Power 5 rosters, the authors find that limits on pay transfer significant resources away from Black students and poorer students and toward White students and wealthier students. In other words, the system is regressive.

How much is transferred away? The authors of the NBER paper calculate that if the student athletes were able to collectively bargain for wages, the median Power

5 football player would receive—wait for it! about
$360,000 a year. To be
sure, the money would be
heavily weighted toward
the most valuable players
on the field. The starting

The NCAA has promised a 2021 vote on whether to funnel more money to players, but opposes any change that would treat players as employees.

quarterback, for example, would earn around $2.4 million. But even backups would
receive about $140,000 each. Cut these estimates in half and the amount of exploi-
tation remains enormous.

The Power 5 conferences certainly have the money to pay football players for
their labor. They just use it for other things. A few years ago, Auburn University
spent nearly $14 million on a five-story-high scoreboard so bright that on a clear
night the glow can be seen 30 miles away. Texas A&M renovated its football stadium
at a cost of nearly half a billion dollars.

One might argue that if the money goes to the players directly rather than into
fancier stadiums, fans will be less likely to attend. I'm skeptical. If true, however,
this claim would provide further evidence that the college football cartel is systematically undercompensating its players. Here's an analogy: Imagine a restaurant
everybody loves because the decor is fancy, the portions are sumptuous, and the
prices are low. What would happen if we discovered that to keep everything so fancy
and cheap for the diners, the owners paid the workers nothing more than expense
money? We'd all be furious.

Supporters of the current system offer a variety of arguments, including the
claim that paying college athletes would risk erosion of the connection between
the players and the values of the institution where they're enrolled. But perhaps the
most common objection to paying collegiate athletes is that the scholarship itself is
adequate compensation. The data remain unclear on whether college athletes as a
group earn the same as other graduates. Still, if the tuition and other perks reflect
the correct compensation for the services of student athletes, no school will offer
more. Thus, the existence of a rule limiting compensation is itself evidence that the
value to the school of the services the players provide is greater than the amount of
the scholarship.

A counterargument is that until they are eligible to be drafted by a professional
club, college athletes are "not worth a single cent on the open market." This has
the problem backwards. There is no open market. Every other business can bid for
the services of labor. Only by allowing college teams to do the same would we learn
what the players are worth.

The NCAA has promised a 2021 vote on whether to funnel more money to
players, but opposes any change that would treat players as employees. The group
also insists that limiting the compensation paid to college football players increases
competitive balance. Studies have found no empirical support for this proposition.

Besides, even if the wealthiest schools would indeed collect all the best players,
that's not enough reason to preserve the regressive system that the NCAA is fighting

so hard to protect. Sanderson and Siegfried suggest that compensating the players at market rates would lead a significant number of schools to give up football. Perhaps only the Power 5 would be left. As a fan, I'd find that painful—but not as painful as a system in which colleges profit from the unpaid labor of students.

Print Citations

CMS: Carter, Stephen L. "Paying College Football Players Is Only Fair." In *The Reference Shelf: College Sports,* edited by Micah L. Issitt, 160-162. Amenia, NY: Grey House Publishing, 2021.

MLA: Carter, Stephen L. "Paying College Football Players Is Only Fair." *The Reference Shelf: College Sports,* edited by Micah L. Issitt, Grey House Publishing, 2021, pp. 160-162.

APA: Carter, S. L. (2021). Paying college football players is only fair. In Micah L. Issitt (Ed.), *The reference shelf College sports* (pp. 160-162). Amenia, NY: Grey House Publishing.

An Argument for Not Allowing College Athletes to Earn Compensation

By Mary Louise Kelley
NPR, October 30, 2019

MARY LOUISE KELLY, HOST:

The NCAA makes close to a billion dollars in revenue each school year, but college players see none of that money. Now that might change. Yesterday, the NCAA's Board of Governors voted to permit student-athletes to benefit from the use of their name, image and likeness. Now, some see this as addressing an unfair practice of exploitative behavior by the NCAA. Others see this as a lousy idea.

Here to discuss is Ekow Yankah. He's a professor at Cardozo School of Law. He has written about this, an essay in The New Yorker back in 2015 titled "Why NCAA Athletes Shouldn't Be Paid." He joins me now from London.

Welcome to ALL THINGS CONSIDERED.

EKOW YANKAH: Thank you for having me.

KELLY: What did you make of this announcement yesterday?

YANKAH: Like most people, we're all sort of waiting to see what the announcement means. The NCAA often tries to do the vaguely right thing when it has absolutely no other choice. So, I take it that this is a capitulation of what they see coming down the pike in terms of a slew of laws that are passing from state to state and threatened federal action.

KELLY: But I gather you think this is a lousy idea. You're in the lousy idea camp. How come?

YANKAH: Well, I'm torn about the name and likeness issue, which is slightly different than paying the athletes. But at bottom, the reason I'm concerned is because I think this will be awfully hard to distinguish from salaries. I consistently worry about the continued professionalization of college athletics.

Look; there's no question that the current system is deeply exploitative and deeply problematic. I guess my baseline worry is many people—I think people in good faith—see the exploitation, and they say the answer is to pay these young athletes some amount of money while they're playing football or basketball. I look, and I say the answer is to make sure that these young men—and with the revenue generated in sports, it's typically young men—that they get the thing that they were promised that was of value. That is to say they get a college degree that was of value.

> **The listeners to NPR, those who have opportunity and resources—how many of them would trade a college degree for their child for three years of their child being in pain in college?**

And one of the things I worry about is how many of, at least the listeners to *NPR*, those who have opportunity and resources—how many of them would trade a college degree for their child for three years of their child being paid in college? I doubt that's a trade that your listeners would make. Those are not the dreams I have for my children.

KELLY: So in your view, should anything change in the current system?

YANKAH: Yeah. I think everybody agrees that the current system needs to be changed and that the corruption of the current system is untenable and, indeed, deeply racially scarred. I'm not interested in whether or not even my beloved Wolverines crank out three or four professionals a year. I'm interested in universities that can crank out generations of black lawyers and doctors and engineers.

It seems to me that the best way to make sure that we are actually serving these young men is to do our best to support and create a true minor league system.

KELLY: Similar to the way it works in Europe already.

YANKAH: Similar to the way it works in Europe. Young kids who want to play for Manchester United are playing in soccer camps from when they're young. Every year, they get cut down. But the ones who dream of playing on the big stage pursue through the minor league system—and similar to the way it works in baseball and, by the way, similar to the way it works in hockey in the United States.

KELLY: I want to make this personal. You played soccer a little bit in college. New college athlete—would you have wanted to get paid?

YANKAH: Maybe in this way I'm a little bit pushed the other way. I played very briefly when Michigan was a club team. In order to keep playing, I would've had to pay money to play. I was working a full-time job in college on top of scholarships. I would've been thrilled to be able to play, just not to pay. And so in this way, I am one of the people who truly thinks that sports are actually a part of an education. You know, we don't think of the dancers as not students, and we don't think of the chess players as not students.

KELLY: The chess team isn't bringing in a billion dollars every year, though.

YANKAH: No, that's true. That's absolutely right. And I think, you know, that's a concern. On the other hand, if there was a true professional league where the students who wanted to make their money could go make their money, then the university could look the student-athletes in the eye and be quite clear that the revenue generation was more about the university than any particular student-athlete. That is to say if your skills are the kind for which you can get paid, you can go to the minor league and get paid.

KELLY: That's Ekow Yankah. He is a professor at Cardozo School of Law, and he wrote an essay for *the New Yorker* titled "Why NCAA Athletes Shouldn't Be Paid."

Ekow Yankah, thanks.

YANKAH: Thank you for having me.

Print Citations

CMS: Kelley, Mary Louise. "An Argument for Not Allowing College Athletes to Earn Compensation." In *The Reference Shelf: College Sports,* edited by Micah L. Issitt, 163-165. Amenia, NY: Grey House Publishing, 2021.

MLA: Kelley, Mary Louise. "An Argument for Not Allowing College Athletes to Earn Compensation." *The Reference Shelf: College Sports,* edited by Micah L. Issitt, Grey House Publishing, 2021, pp. 163-165.

APA: Kelley, M. L. (2021). An argument for not allowing college athletes to earn compensation. In Micah L. Issitt (Ed.), *The reference shelf: College sports* (pp. 163-165). Amenia, NY: Grey House Publishing.

Overtime Is Starting a Basketball League for 16- to-18-Year-Olds That Pays at Least $100,000 a Year

By Jabari Young
CNBC, March 8, 2021

Is Overtime CEO Dan Porter losing his mind?

The sports company's co-founder recalled that reaction from former National Basketball Association Commissioner David Stern when he pitched establishing another hoops league.

Overtime announced on Thursday that it plans to start a basketball league for 16-to-18-year-olds allowing them to earn at least $100,000 per year.

The Overtime Elite (OTE) league will let players bypass traditional high school and collegiate levels while building their brand before becoming eligible for the NBA. It will start in September with 30 players, and will be based in a single location, which is still under discussion.

The News with Shepard Smith

In an interview Wednesday, Porter confirmed Overtime would pay all health insurance and allow players to earn bonuses and equity in Overtime. He also recalled the Stern's skepticism.

"It's a pretty interesting opportunity," Porter said of starting OTE.

Overtime distributes original sports content on social media outlets, including Snapchat, Google-owned YouTube, and Facebook-owned Instagram, and sells apparel with its logos and branding. Most of the content revolves around high school or other amateur players, but it does not license highlights or material from major sports leagues.

Porter and Zachary Weiner, both former William Morris Endeavor executives, founded Overtime in 2016 with investments from Stern and others.

Since then, the company has built a massive Generation Z following from high school basketball players. The company has over 40 million followers across its social media channels and has built credibility among NBA stars like Zion Williamson and Atlanta Hawks point guard Trae Young.

The company says its content is streamed more than 1.7 billion times a month across all social platforms—mostly by Gen Z. Polls have suggested this group of

13-to-24-year-olders prefers highlights and quick sports content over traditional formats, and they favor basketball over other sports.

Overtime's revenue comes from two sources. One is indirectly aligning with brands by integrating them into its content and making money off video ads. The other is direct revenue via e-commerce, where Porter says the company makes "millions of dollars" from apparel.

"Just like a sports team when you buy a hat or jersey," Porter said, "people feel a part of that community, and they buy apparel to represent that. We think there is a big opportunity to lean into what is at the core of basketball for young people and create an apparel brand."

Overtime declined to disclose its financials.

With OTE, Porter expects the revenue model to change a bit "from e-commerce and media to e-commerce, media, rights and licensing much like a league." He said OTE eventually wants to sell its media rights.

"Not early on. We're going to take our time," Porter said.

Overtime is also engaged in active talks for brand partners and distribution for the league.

A New Basketball Farm System?

Porter said he spent two years speaking with families of top athletes to seek input about OTE. He said the families expressed disapproval of the current path to the pros, where prominent colleges make millions off talent in exchange for a free education.

OTE says it will provide top education, residences and training and will offer advanced analytics of players' performance to help them improve. But the big advantage is that OTE will give players the right to capitalize on their brands while getting paid to participate.

"We are the only country in the world that forces you to go to high school and then go to college to become a pro athlete, at least in basketball and football," Porter said.

As part of its collective bargaining agreement, the NBA prohibits players under age 19 from entering the league. Some players attend at least one year of college while they await eligibility; hence, the popular "one and done" term.

Porter referenced players like former NBA guard Brandon Jennings and Charlotte Hornets guard LaMelo Ball, who both bypassed college.

> **The Overtime Elite (OTE) league will let players bypass traditional high school and collegiate levels while building their brand before becoming eligible for the NBA.**

"We're doing it based on the observation of how these young athletes are trying to change the system and make it work for them," said Porter.

"We are a big platform, and that makes us a good place to go out and find talent," Porter said. "We're starting a league from scratch. We don't have any legacy overhang. We can build a model that feels like a 21st century model both in terms of how start-ups and how digital companies are created."

Porter said OTE could serve as a new pathway to the NBA. The NBA already has a noncollege route with its NBA G League Ignite program, featuring top high school prospects Jalen Green and Isaiah Todd. This route allows younger players to train in the program until they become eligible.

Players in the NBA's program are paid between $200,000 and $500,000 while they await eligibility.

Should OTE players not pursue a professional career, it will provide an additional $100,000 for college tuition. But if youths do participate in the league, players lose their NCAA eligibility because they are receiving payment.

"It's a professional path," Porter said. "But unlike a pure farm system, this is competition. We expect tens of millions of people will want to tune in and watch. And why do we expect that? Because they are already watching on our platforms today."

Portland Trail Blazers forward Carmelo Anthony, an OTE investor and board member, said many athletes aren't properly prepared for the life of a professional athlete.

"We need to do a better job of empowering the next generation of players and setting them up for success," he said. "OTE is leading the way on that front by offering players a comprehensive route that fully develops the athlete—not just basketball skills, but education, economic empowerment and building their own brand. Having this type of guidance for high school players is critical in setting them up for a successful career, both on and off the court."

Seeking Approval

Porter said early reaction around the league is positive, and it's built with NBA names that can help OTE operate efficiently.

In addition to Anthony, investors include Brooklyn Nets star Kevin Durant and Silicon Valley venture capital firm Andreessen Horowitz. The commissioner is former NBA executive Aaron Ryan, and ex-Sacramento Kings assistant general manager Brandon Williams will oversee league operations.

"There is a lot of NBA DNA in this," Porter said.

But Stern was the most influential. He was the first investor in Overtime, helping it raise $2.5 million in 2017, three years before his death.

Porter remembered Stern telling him to avoid starting a league. "I spent 30 years doing this. You do not want to do something like this," Porter recalled him saying.

"But we're annoyingly persistent," he added.

As Stern watched Overtime take off among Gen Z, he became convinced that OTE was a good idea and approved of it, Porter said.

"He said, 'I think not only can you guys do this, but you need to do this,'" recalled Porter. "We were like wow. That's like a 180. That's when we felt we could do this. When you build a company in this world, you can't count on people giving you opportunities," Porter added. "You have to make your own way."

Print Citations

CMS: Young, Jabari. "Overtime Is Starting a Basketball League for 16- to-18-Year-Olds That Pays at Least $100,000 a Year." In *The Reference Shelf: College Sports,* edited by Micah L. Issitt, 166-169. Amenia, NY: Grey House Publishing, 2021.

MLA: Young, Jabari. "Overtime Is Starting a Basketball League for 16- to-18-Year-Olds That Pays at Least $100,000 a Year." *The Reference Shelf: College Sports,* edited by Micah L. Issitt, Grey House Publishing, 2021, pp. 166-169.

APA: Young, J. (2021). Overtime is starting a basketball league for 16- to-18-year-olds that pays at least $100,000 a year. In Micah L. Issitt (Ed.), *The reference shelf: College sports* (pp. 166-169). Amenia, NY: Grey House Publishing.

Supreme Court Will Hear NCAA Case on College Athlete Pay; The Case Could Upend the College Sports Business Model

By Leah Nylen and Juan Perez Jr.
Politico, December 16, 2020

The Supreme Court will hear a landmark antitrust case against the NCAA that could upend the business model for college sports by allowing colleges to compensate student athletes.

The high court said Wednesday that it will hear appeals filed by the NCAA and one of its member conferences over a May decision that found the group's limits on player compensation violate antitrust law.

In its petition to the justices, the NCAA accused the lower courts of "judicial micromangement" and said their rulings would fundamentally transform college sports by blurring "the traditional line between college and professional athletes."

"We are pleased the U.S. Supreme Court will review the NCAA's right to provide student-athletes with the educational benefits they need to succeed in school and beyond," Donald Remy, the NCAA's chief legal officer, said in a statement. "The NCAA and its members continue to believe that college campuses should be able to improve the student-athlete experience without facing never-ending litigation regarding these changes."

One advocate for college athletes suggested, however, that the Supreme Court could rule even more favorably for players.

"This gives college athletes the chance to not only solidify the win in the lower courts, but the Supreme Court may decide the lower courts didn't go far enough in allowing athlete compensation," said Ramogi Huma, a former UCLA football player who now leads the National College Players Association advocacy group.

Background: The high court declined in August to pause the earlier court rulings while the NCAA's Supreme Court petition was under review.

A group of current and former players challenged the NCAA rules that prohibit athletes from accepting money or other forms of compensation. Following a 2019 trial, a federal judge found the restrictions anti-competitive and said the NCAA must allow colleges to offer student athletes education-related benefits, such as graduate school scholarships, study abroad opportunities or computers for educational use.

The U.S. Court of Appeals for the 9th Circuit affirmed that decision earlier this year.

Pending legislation: More than two dozen states have introduced or debated legislation that would allow athletes to profit from their personal brands. But the NCAA wants federal protection to quash those efforts and set its own standards for more than 1,200 schools.

In Congress, Democrats are setting out a much different framework for the future of college sports. Advertised as a "College Athletes Bill of Rights," a Democratic outline of forthcoming legislation has proposed paying student athletes through revenue-sharing agreements with athletic associations, conferences and schools that make money off college sports. The proposal also would allow athletes to pitch products or services for their own profit.

> **More than two dozen states have introduced or debate legislation that would allow athletes to profit from their personal brands.**

A bill from Senate Commerce Chair Roger Wicker (R-Miss.) would instead fulfill much of the NCAA's wishlist by overriding state laws and allowing the federal government to control rules on how college athletes might earn money from endorsement deals or signing autographs.

Wicker's measure would allow athletes to earn money from their "name, image and likeness," under a series of restrictions, and authorize the Federal Trade Commission to choose a private entity—which could include the NCAA—to develop and enforce those rules. The legislation would also shield schools, athletic conferences and the NCAA from liability to any federal and state laws relating to trade and competition.

Reps. Anthony Gonzalez (R-Ohio) and Emanuel Cleaver (D-Mo.) have introduced similar legislation in the House. A related proposal from Sen. Marco Rubio (R-Fla.) has also won plaudits from the NCAA.

What's next: The Supreme Court will hear arguments in the case in the spring, likely in March or April. The justices will issue a decision before the current term ends in June.

Print Citations

CMS: Nylen, Leah, and Juan Perez, Jr. "Supreme Court Will Hear NCAA Case on College Athlete Pay: The Case Could Upend the College Sports Business Model." In *The Reference Shelf: College Sports,* edited by Micah L. Issitt, 170-172. Amenia, NY: Grey House Publishing, 2021.

MLA: Nylen, Leah, and Juan Perez, Jr. "Supreme Court Will Hear NCAA Case on College Athlete Pay: The Case Could Upend the College Sports Business Model." *The Reference*

Shelf: College Sports, edited by Micah L. Issitt, Grey House Publishing, 2021, pp. 170-172.

APA: Nylen, L., & Perez, Jr., J. (2021). Supreme Court will hear NCAA case on college athlete pay: The case could upend the college sports business model. In Micah L. Issitt (Ed.), *The reference shelf: College sports* (pp. 170-172). Amenia, NY: Grey House Publishing.

Harvard, Local Universities Oppose College Sports Gambling in Letter to State House

By Michelle G. Kurilla and Ema R. Schumer
The Harvard Crimson, November 14, 2020

Harvard and six other local colleges and universities opposed a bill that would legalize college sports betting in a Friday letter to Massachusetts state legislators.

The presidents and athletic directors of Boston College, Boston University, the College of the Holy Cross, Merrimack College, Northeastern University, the University of Massachusetts, and Harvard University signed onto the letter, which was addressed to Massachusetts Senate President Karen E. Spilka, Speaker of the House Robert A. DeLeo, Senator Michael J. Rodrigues, Senator Eric P. Lesser '07, Senator Patrick M. O'Connor, Representative Ann-Margaret Ferrante, Representative Aaron Michlewitz, and Representative Donald H. Wong.

The signatories of the letter, including University President Lawrence S. Bacow and Harvard Athletics Director Erin McDermott, expressed their opposition to a provision in House Bill 488—a bill introduced to spur economic development in the Commonwealth—that seeks to legalize sports betting, including on college athletics competitions. The House of Representatives voted in favor of the provision in late July, though the Senate voted against amendments that would have included the provision in the legislation.

"Based on our years of experience, each of us believes that such legislation will create unnecessary and unacceptable risks to student athletes, their campus peers, and the integrity and culture of colleges and universities in the Commonwealth," the letter reads.

University administrators laid out their opposition to legalized college betting on the grounds that it could compromise the integrity of student-athlete competition, promote unhealthy and financially risky habits among students, and deplete limited university resources.

"Easy access to placing bets can lead to bad decisions and even addictive behavior in regard to making wagers on 'big games,' creating mental health and financial problems for students and their families," the letter reads.

Legalized gambling could impose pressure on student-athletes to sway game outcomes, the letter cautions.

"Student athletes could be persuaded that agreeing to limit scoring or committing an 'unforced' error would not really matter," they wrote. "But doing so clearly harms personal and institutional values, has no place in college sports, and, as history shows, often leads to more corrupt and unethical actions."

> **Legalized gambling could impose pressure on student-athletes to sway game outcomes.**

Gambling on college sports could also incentivize students to share information regarding their classmates who are varsity athletes—including their health and playing status—with gamblers who would benefit from such knowledge, according to the letter.

They wrote that, on an institutional level, the legalization of gambling in college sports would financially strain university resources as schools enforce athletics policies. They added university leaders would have to "devote more scarce time and resources to protecting the brand, values, image, and reputation of their schools."

"We recognize that during the current difficult economic climate, the Legislature desires to develop new sources of revenue, including sports wagering," the letter concludes. "But like other states, Massachusetts can gain those benefits without legalizing college sports betting. Such a limitation is necessary to safeguard the longstanding distinctive role and contribution of student-athletes as well as to preserve the integrity of intercollegiate athletics in the Commonwealth."

Print Citations

CMS: Kurilla, Michelle G., and Ema R. Schumer. "Harvard, Local Universities Oppose College Sports Gambling in Letter to State House." In *The Reference Shelf: College Sports,* edited by Micah L. Issitt, 173-174. Amenia, NY: Grey House Publishing, 2021.

MLA: Kurilla, Michelle G., and Ema R. Schumer. "Harvard, Local Universities Oppose College Sports Gambling in Letter to State House." *The Reference Shelf: College Sports,* edited by Micah L. Issitt, Grey House Publishing, 2021, pp. 173-174.

APA: Kurilla, M. G., & Schumer, E. R. (2021). Harvard, local universities oppose college sports gambling in letter to state house. In Micah L. Issitt (Ed.), *The reference shelf: College sports* (pp. 173-174). Amenia, NY: Grey House Publishing.

The NCAA Faces a Full Court Press

By Leah Nylen, Juan Perez Jr., and Julia Arciga
Politico, March 31, 2021

The National Collegiate Athletic Association—amid a social media onslaught during its men's and women's basketball tournament—is under scrutiny at the Supreme Court on Wednesday as a broader athletes' rights movement seeks to shape the organization's future.

The Supreme Court will focus on whether the NCAA's hard limits on athlete compensation violate antitrust law, not the policy debate on player endorsements smoldering inside Capitol Hill, statehouses and stadiums. The high court hearing is just one of a bevy of problems the group—founded exactly 115 years ago Wednesday after a rash of football injuries and deaths—faces as it deals with renewed questions about fair labor and equity between men's and women's sports.

"This is a civil rights issue," said Jordan Bohannon, a redshirt senior guard on the University of Iowa's men's basketball tournament team who has helped lead the #NotNCAAProperty protest.

"The fact of the matter is college athletes are the only ones that get limited. We have a certain cap on what we can receive. It's not fair, and it's not equal."

College athletics is enmeshed in a transformative moment as lawmakers in Congress and statehouses weigh new laws to allow athletes to profit from personal endorsements and sponsorships.

"We need the same basic rights as other students," Bohannon said in an interview. "Especially those of us participating in this tournament that is making close to a billion dollars" for the NCAA.

The players have won significant attention. Bohannon said a group of athletes plan to meet with NCAA President Mark Emmert, Sen. Cory Booker (D-N.J.) and potentially representatives from the Biden administration on Thursday morning.

They may find a willing ear in the Biden administration. After staying mum for most of the litigation between the NCAA and student-athletes, the Justice Department sided with the players earlier this month in the court case being heard Wednesday. It was the department's first foray into the case at the intersection of antitrust and labor rights. DOJ's acting Solicitor General Elizabeth Prelogar will argue in support of the players at Wednesday's Supreme Court hearing.

The antitrust case represents a fundamental threat to the athletic association's business model, one playing out while the NCAA and powerful college sports conferences lobby Congress to regulate how players can sign third-party endorsements.

The decision could open a new frontier in college sports. For the NCAA, a victory would allow the organization to better fend off a barrage of lawsuits that have already helped loosen its internal rules on the benefits colleges can give players. If the athletic association loses, student athletes are expected to gain a flood of new money from schools that profit off their work.

It's hard to square the NCAA's more than $1 billion in annual revenue with stories about former University of Connecticut basketball star Shabazz Napier going to bed "starving" because NCAA's restrictions meant he didn't have money for food, said Maureen Weston, a law professor at Pepperdine University.

"It's on the backs of these star athletes that college sports is operating," said Weston, who heads Pepperdine's entertainment, media and sports law program. "The practical issues are how to implement [compensation rules] and how does it impact the NCAA's responsibilities for fairness to all athletes?"

> **If the athletic association loses, student athletes are expected to gain a flood of new money from schools that profit off work.**

As college basketball players compete in a multibillion dollar tournament, the Supreme Court hears oral arguments today in a case that could shift the way the NCAA regulates compensation for those athletes.

The NCAA's commitment to providing equal opportunity and access to all athletes has also come under fire.

Last week, the NCAA publicly apologized to women's basketball players after outcry on social media led by Oregon Ducks' Sedona Prince over the stark discrepancy in the men's and women's weight rooms.

The social media posts prompted more than 30 members of Congress to demand answers from the NCAA on the apparent unequal treatment. University of South Carolina head coach Dawn Staley said the incident shows the NCAA does not think "the women's players 'deserve' the same amenities" the men have.

"Women's basketball is a popular sport whose stock and presence continues to rise on a global level," she wrote in a statement. "It is sad that the NCAA is not willing to recognize and invest in our growth despite its claims of togetherness and equality."

The NCAA has now hired a law firm to review gender-equity concerns about its tournaments since federal civil rights law prohibits discrimination in college sports, including equal access to equipment and supplies.

At the Supreme Court, the NCAA is appealing a lower court decision that ruled the association must let schools offer costly educational benefits and even cash awards for student athletes. The association and its attorneys have pressed justices to protect the organization's governance model for roughly 1,200 member schools and athletic conferences, and argued that the lower court ruling distorts federal antitrust law.

"The ruling also encourages judicial micromanagement and invites never-ending litigation as the NCAA seeks to improve the college athletic experience," said Donald Remy, the NCAA's chief legal officer, in a statement last month. "In short, the lower court ruling greatly blurs the line between college and professional sports."

Bohannon, from Iowa, believes the NCAA's current structure devalues college athletes. "I know they're a nonprofit organization," he said. "But I believe they're a huge corporation that continues to do things that are for their own self-interest, and not the interests of the college athletes that they have always prided themselves on for decades and decades."

Bohannon isn't alone. More than a dozen groups, including those representing NFL, NBA, WNBA and Women's Soccer players, former NCAA executives, and Arizona, New York and six other states, weighed in to support the student-athletes.

Pepperdine's Weston, who has spent the past two decades focused on the NCAA and its policies, said what the organization looks like a year from now could be completely different.

"You could say the NCAA is having near-death experience," she said.

Print Citations

CMS: Nylen, L., Juan Perez, Jr., and Julia Arciga. "The NCAA Faces a Full Court Press." In *The Reference Shelf: College Sports,* edited by Micah L. Issitt, 175-177. Amenia, NY: Grey House Publishing, 2021.

MLA: Nylen, L., Juan Perez, Jr., and Julia Arciga. "The NCAA Faces a Full Court Press." *The Reference Shelf: College Sports,* edited by Micah L. Issitt, Grey House, 2021, pp. 175-177.

APA: Nylen, L., Perez, Jr., J., & Arciga, J. (2021). The NCAA faces a full court press. In Micah L. Issitt (Ed.), *The reference shelf: College sports* (pp. 175-177). Amenia, NY: Grey House Publishing.

Supreme Court Rules Against Restrictions on Colleges Offering Educational Perks to Compensate Student-Athletes

By Robert Barnes and Molly Hensley-Clancy
The Washington Post, June 21, 2021

The Supreme Court ruled unanimously Monday against the NCAA's limits on education-related perks for college athletes, a serious blow to the organization's power to dictate the rules for compensating those who participate in college sports.

In a 9-to-0 vote, the court rejected the National Collegiate Athletic Association's argument that its rules limiting such educational benefits were necessary to preserve the image of amateurism in college sports.

The ruling itself was narrow, and it did not concern the question of paying students for their athletic prowess. But Justice Brett M. Kavanaugh, in a separate opinion, anticipated that as a next step, and warned that the "NCAA's business model would be flatly illegal in almost any other industry in America."

The "bottom line," he wrote, "is that the NCAA and its member colleges are suppressing the pay of student athletes who collectively generate billions of dollars in revenues for colleges every year."

The biggest takeaway from the court's action, experts said, might be that the court is no longer accepting of the NCAA's argument that it has a unique role to play in protecting the amateur status of college sports, and deserves special dispensation from antitrust laws.

"The notion of NCAA exceptionalism is dead, or at least, on significant life support," said Dionne Koller, a law professor and the director of the Center for Sport and the Law at the University of Baltimore.

High school sports will feel impact of athlete branding changes. For some, that's cause for concern.

The ruling comes amid a sea change in the world of college sports that has shifted the tide rapidly against the NCAA when it comes to athletes' rights.

The NCAA has been left scrambling to deal with laws in dozens of states that will allow athletes the right to make money off their own name, image and likeness — the first of which takes effect July 1. Congress and state lawmakers have started a push to give college athletes even broader rights, such as the ability to unionize or demand a share of their sport's revenue.

And the college sports behemoth is also fighting a battle on issues of gender equity after an onslaught of criticism over its treatment of women athletes.

> **The ruling comes amid a sea change in the world of college sports that has shifted the tide rapidly against the NCAA when it comes to athletes' rights.**

The NCAA has asked Congress to pass name, image and likeness legislation that would go into effect nationally. But it wants a limited exemption to antitrust laws as part of that legislation—a demand that is likely to face even more-serious opposition in the wake of the Supreme Court's ruling.

The NCAA was contesting a lower-court ruling that allowed colleges to offer greater academic-related enticements to Division I football and men's and women's basketball players—benefits such as scholarships for graduate degrees, paid postgraduate internships, and provision of free computers, musical instruments and other types of equipment related to education.

The NCAA generally limits benefits to scholarships and the cost of attending college. It warned that providing more leeway to promise greater benefits could lead to internships with boosters and athletic companies that offered extravagant salaries as a "thinly disguised vehicle" for paying professional-level salaries.

Protecting the amateur nature of college athletics is paramount in protecting its brand, the NCAA argued, and what separates it from professional sports.

The decision came in a long-running antitrust lawsuit filed by former West Virginia running back Shawne Alston and former University of California center Justine Hartman, representing a class of former men's and women's college athletes.

U.S. District Judge Claudia Wilken agreed with the NCAA about direct compensation. But she said enhanced education benefits were fair game, even though the NCAA said it would set up a bidding war between universities and athletic conferences for top athletes.

Justice Neil M. Gorsuch, writing for the court, said Wilken had carefully examined the NCAA's case and found it did not make a compelling argument for why the organization should be spared from the normal rigor of antitrust litigation.

The lower-court decision "stands on firm ground—an exhaustive factual record, a thoughtful legal analysis consistent with established antitrust principles, and a healthy dose of judicial humility," Gorsuch wrote.

Gorsuch acknowledged that the court in a 1984 case called *NCAA v. Board of Regents* said the NCAA played a unique role that courts should consider when assessing whether its actions violate the antitrust Sherman Act. But that goes only so far, he wrote.

"Given the sensitivity of antitrust analysis to market realities—and how much has changed in this market—we think it would be particularly unwise to treat an aside in Board of Regents as more than that," he wrote.

The NCAA's lawyer told the Supreme Court during oral arguments that the decision, upheld by the U.S. Court of Appeals for the 9th Circuit, approves "a regime that permits athletes to be paid thousands of dollars each year just for playing on a team and unlimited cash for post-eligibility internships."

In a statement after the ruling, the organization emphasized the power the opinion said it retains.

"While today's decision preserves the lower court ruling, it also reaffirms the NCAA's authority to adopt reasonable rules and repeatedly notes that the NCAA remains free to articulate what are and are not truly educational benefits, consistent with the NCAA's mission to support student-athletes," the statement said.

"Even though the decision does not directly address name, image and likeness, the NCAA remains committed to supporting NIL benefits for student-athletes," said NCAA President Mark Emmert. "Additionally, we remain committed to working with Congress to chart a path forward, which is a point the Supreme Court expressly stated in its ruling."

But the reaction elsewhere was that the opinion marked a definitive change.

"The NCAA is now fighting with one hand behind their backs," said Michael Carrier, a professor at Rutgers University who filed an amicus brief in the case in favor of college athletes.

"The amateurism defense, on which the NCAA has relied for decades, is now riddled with holes," Carrier said. "For any litigation down the road in which student-athletes seek more than they did in this case, the NCAA is going to have a very difficult time."

The Biden administration sided with the players, saying the lower-court decision was carefully crafted to allow only payments related to education.

Both Gorsuch and Kavanaugh mentioned the billions of dollars at stake, which they said benefited the NCAA, the universities and the coaches, but not the student-athletes.

"Those who run this enterprise profit in a different way than the student-athletes whose activities they oversee," Gorsuch wrote. "The president of the NCAA earns nearly $4 million per year ... and annual salaries for top Division I college football coaches approach $11 million."

Gorsuch said that it was puzzling that the NCAA had appealed the lower-court ruling, and that it was "unclear exactly what the NCAA seeks." If it is that the court should overlook restrictions on a monopoly "because they happen to fall at the intersection of higher education, sports, and money—we cannot agree."

He added that the lower-court decision gave the organization power to regulate the benefits colleges offer. "The NCAA is free to forbid in-kind benefits unrelated to a student's actual education; nothing stops it from enforcing a 'no Lamborghini' rule," Gorsuch wrote.

Kavanaugh's concurring opinion was scorching: "College presidents, athletic directors, coaches, conference commissioners, and NCAA executives take in six- and seven-figure salaries. Colleges build lavish new facilities. But the student athletes who generate the revenues, many of whom are African American and from lower-income backgrounds, end up with little or nothing."

That said, Kavanaugh acknowledged the difficulty of compensating athletes in sports other than revenue-generators such as football and basketball. He noted there are about 180,000 Division I student-athletes.

"What is a financially sustainable way of fairly compensating some or all of those student athletes?" he asked.

The case is *NCAA v. Alston*.

Print Citations

CMS: Barnes, Robert, and Molly Hensley-Clancy. "Supreme Court Rules Against Restrictions on Colleges Offering Educational Perks to Compensate Student-Athletes." In *The Reference Shelf: College Sports,* edited by Micah L. Issitt, 178-181. Amenia, NY: Grey House Publishing, 2021.

MLA: Barnes, Robert, and Molly Hensley-Clancy. "Supreme Court Rules Against Restrictions on Colleges Offering Educational Perks to Compensate Student-Athletes." *The Reference Shelf: College Sports,* edited by Micah L. Issitt, Grey House Publishing, 2021, pp. 178-181.

APA: Barnes, Robert, and Molly Hensley-Clancy. (2021). Supreme court rules against restrictions on colleges offering educational perks to compensate student-athletes . In Micah L. Issitt (Ed.), *The reference shelf: College sports* (pp. 178-181). Amenia, NY: Grey House Publishing.

Bibliography

Adelson, Andrea. "Survey: Coaches, Athletes Think Racism Is an Issue." *ESPN*. Oct 14, 2020. https://www.espn.com/college-sports/story/_/id/30116337/coaches-athletes-feel-need-act-racism. Accessed 27 May 2021.

"Average per Athlete 2020." *Scholarship Stats*. 2021. https://scholarshipstats.com/average-per-athlete. Accessed 15 May 2021.

Bell, Richard C. "A History of Women in Sport Prior to Title IX." *The Sport Journal*. https://thesportjournal.org/article/a-history-of-women-in-sport-prior-to-title-ix/. Accessed 18 May 2021.

Berkowitz, Steve. "NCAA Reports Revenues of More Than $1 Billion in 2017." *USA Today*. Mar 7, 2018. https://www.usatoday.com/story/sports/college/2018/03/07/ncaa-reports-revenues-more-than-1-billion-2017/402486002/. Accessed 27 May 2021.

Berkowitz, S., and C. Schnaars. "Colleges Are Spending More on Their Athletes because They Can." *USA Today*. Jul 6, 2017. https://www.usatoday.com/story/sports/college/2017/07/06/colleges-spending-more-their-athletes-because-they-can/449433001/. Accessed 15, May 2021.

Berkowitz, Steve, Lindsay Schnell, and Dan Wolken. "'I Assumed They Were Treating Us Fairly': Why Can't NCAA Get Women's Basketball Right?" *USA Sports*. Mar 27, 2021. https://www.usatoday.com/in-depth/sports/ncaaw/2021/03/27/march-madness-why-cant-ncaa-get-womens-basketball-right/7012017002/. Accessed 27 May 2021.

Berkowitz, S., and T. Schad. "5 Surprising Findings from College Football Coaches Salaries Report." *USA Today*. Oct 14, 2020. https://www.usatoday.com/story/sports/ncaaf/2020/10/14/college-football-coaches-salaries-five-surprising-findings-data/5900066002/. Accessed 15 May 2021.

Billitz, Jess. "19 College Athlete Injury Statistics (The Risk of Sports)." *Noobgains*. Nov 12, 2020. https://noobgains.com/college-athlete-injury-statistics/. Accessed 18 May 2021.

Branch, Taylor. "The Shame of College Sports." *The Atlantic*. Oct 2011. https://www.theatlantic.com/magazine/archive/2011/10/the-shame-of-college-sports/308643/. Accessed 25 May 2021.

Davis, Timothy. "The Myth of the Superspade: The Persistence of Racism in College Athletics." *Fordham Urban Law Journal*. Vol. 22, No. 3 (1995). https://ir.lawnet.fordham.edu/cgi/viewcontent.cgi?article=1664&context=ulj&httpsredir=1&referer=. Accessed 18 May 2021.

Drozdowski, Mark J. "Do Colleges Make Money from Athletics?" *Best Colleges*. Nov 16, 2020. https://www.bestcolleges.com/blog/do-college-sports-make-money/. Accessed 15 May 2021.

Farmer, Angela. "Let's Get Real with College Athletes about Their Chances of Going Pro." *The Conversation*. Apr 24, 2019. https://theconversation.com/lets-get-real-with-college-athletes-about-their-chances-of-going-pro-110837. Accessed 26 May 2021.

"Finances of Intercollegiate Athletics Database." *NCAA*. 2019. https://www.ncaa.org/about/resources/research/finances-intercollegiate-athletics-database. Accessed 15 May 2021.

Fixler, Kevin. "The $5 Million Question: Should College Athletes Buy Disability Insurance?" *The Atlantic*. Apr 11, 2013. https://www.theatlantic.com/entertainment/archive/2013/04/the-5-million-question-should-college-athletes-buy-disability-insurance/274915/. Accessed 20 May 2021.

Garthwaite, Criag, Jordan Keener, Matthew J. Notowidigdo, and Nicole F. Ozminkowski. "Who Profits from Amateurism? Rent-Sharing in Modern College Sports." *NBER*. Working Paper 27734. August 2020. https://www.nber.org/system/files/working_papers/w27734/w27734.pdf. Accessed 19 May 2021.

Given, Karen. "Walter Byers: The Man Who Built the NCAA, Then Tried to Tear It Down." *WBUR*. Oct 13, 2017. https://www.wbur.org/onlyagame/2017/10/13/walter-byers-ncaa. Accessed 25 May 2021.

Guy, Lewis. "The Beginning of Organized Collegiate Sport." *American Quarterly*. Vol. 22, No. 2 (Summer, 1970).

Harlan, Jessica. "Lasting Benefits of College Sports for Student Athletes." *Gallup*. Jun 24, 2020. https://news.gallup.com/opinion/gallup/313025/lasting-benefits-college-sports-student-athletes.aspx. Accessed 27 May 2021.

"Heads Up." *CDC*. 2021. https://www.cdc.gov/headsup/basics/concussion_symptoms.html. Accessed 18 May 2021.

Hess, Abigail Johnson. "Meet Chloe V. Mitchell: One of the First College Athletes to Make Money from Her Likeness." *CNBC*. Jan 8, 2021. https://www.cnbc.com/2021/01/08/chloe-v-mitchell-the-first-college-athlete-to-monetize-her-likeness.html. Accessed 25 May 2021.

Higgins, Laine. "Women's College Sports Was Growing: Then the NCAA Took Over." *The Wall Street Journal*. Apr 3, 2021. https://www.wsj.com/articles/women-college-sports-ncaa-aiaw-11617422325. Accessed 18 May 2021.

Hobson, Will, and Steven Rich. "Playing In the Red." *The Washington Post*. Nov 23, 2015. https://www.washingtonpost.com/sf/sports/wp/2015/11/23/running-up-the-bills/?itid=sf_. Accessed 15 May 2021.

Hu, Cynthia. "Non-Revenue Sports Should Not Be Scapegoats for Budget Cuts." *The Johns Hopkins News-Letter*. Oct 22, 2020.

Illing, Sean. "College Football Is a Moneymaking Sham." *Vox*. Sep 5, 2017. https://www.vox.com/conversations/2017/9/5/16180862/college-football-ncaa-student-athlete-mike-mcintire. Accessed 27 May 2021.

Kerr, Zachary Y., et al. "College Sports-Related Injuries–United States, 2009-10 through 2013-14 Academic Years." *Morbidity and Mortality Weekly Report (MMWR)*. Dec 11, 2015. https://www.cdc.gov/mmwr/preview/mmwrhtml/mm6448a2.htm. Accessed 16 May 2021.

"Madness, Inc.: How College Sports Can Leave Athletes Broken and Abandoned." *Chris Murphy*. 2019. https://www.murphy.senate.gov/imo/media/doc/Madness%203...pdf. Accessed 17 May 2021.

Mez, Jesse, Daniel H. Daneshvar, and Patrick T. Kiernan. "Clinicopathological Evaluation of Chronic Traumatic Encephalopathy in Players of American Football." *JAMA*. Jul 25, 2017. https://jamanetwork.com/journals/jama/fullarticle/2645104. Accessed 20 May 2021.

"NCAA Finances." *USA Today*. 2019. https://sports.usatoday.com/ncaa/finances/. Accessed 15 May 2021.

Slama, Remington. "College Sports, Enter at Your Own Risk: An Overview of the NCAA Insurance Policies Available to its Student-Athletes." *Law Review*. Apr 20, 2021. https://lawreview.unl.edu/college-sports-enter-your-own-risk-overview-ncaa-insurance-policies-available-its-student-athletes. Accessed 27 May 2021.

Smith, Ronald A. *Pay for Play: A History of Big-Time College Athletic Reform*. Urbana: University of Illinois Press, 2011.

Smith, Ronald A. *Sports and Freedom: The Rise of Big-Time College Athletics*. New York: Oxford UP, 1988.

Smith, Rodney K. "A Brief History of the National Collegiate Athletic Association's Role in Regulating Intercollegiate Athletics." *Marquette Sports Law Review*. Vol. 11, No. 1 (2000).

Spector, Jesse. "Will Colleges Cover Medical Bills for Athletes Who Get COVID-19? Don't Count on It." *Deadspin*. Jul 02, 2020. https://deadspin.com/will-colleges-cover-medical-bills-for-athletes-who-get-1844251705. Accessed 20 May 2021.

Strauss, Ben, and Molly Hensley-Clancy. "Women's Sports Can Do at Least One Thing Men's Can't, Experts Say: Get Bigger." *The Washington Post*. Apr 1, 2021. https://www.washingtonpost.com/sports/2021/04/01/womens-sports-growth-ratings-business/. Accessed 19 May 2021.

Streeter, Kurt. "College Sports Can Be Exploitative: They Can Also Be a Lifeline." *The New York Times*. Mar 8, 2021. https://www.nytimes.com/2021/03/08/sports/ncaabasketball/athletes-pay-college.html. Accessed 27 May 2021.

"Student Athletes." *At Your Own Risk*. 2019. https://www.atyourownrisk.org/studentathletes/. Accessed 25 May 2021.

Vanover, Eric T., and Michael M. DeBowes. "The Impact of Intercollegiate Athletics in Higher Education." *Academic Perspectives in Higher Education*. 2013. https://www.odu.edu/content/dam/odu/col-dept/efl/docs/intercollegiate-athletics-in-higher-education.pdf. Accessed 15 May 2021.

Walsh, Meghan. "'I Trusted 'Em': When NCAA Schools Abandon Their Injured Athletes." *The Atlantic*. May 1, 2013. https://www.theatlantic.com/entertainment/archive/2013/05/i-trusted-em-when-ncaa-schools-abandon-their-injured-athletes/275407/. Accessed 20 May 2021.

"What Is a Concussion?" *BIRI*. Brain Injury Research Institute. 2021. http://www.

protectthebrain.org/Brain-Injury-Research/What-is-a-Concussion-.aspx.   Accessed 19 May 2021.

"Why Males Pack a Powerful Punch." *Science Daily*. Feb 5, 2020. https://www.sciencedaily.com/releases/2020/02/200205132404.htm#:~:text=It's%20already%20known%20that%20males,%25%20more%20strength%20than%20females'. Accessed 25 May 2021.

Willingham, A. J. "What Is eSports? A Look at an Explosive Billion-Dollar Industry." *CNN*. Aug 27, 2018. https://www.cnn.com/2018/08/27/us/esports-what-is-video-game-professional-league-madden-trnd/index.html. Accessed 25 May 2021.

Winkie, Luke. "Why College Are Betting Big on Video Games." *The Atlantic*. Nov 13, 2019. https://www.theatlantic.com/technology/archive/2019/11/harrisburg-university-esports-players-are-only-athletes/601840/. Accessed 25 May 2021.

Websites

College Athlete Advocacy Initiative

www.4collegeathletes.org

The College Athlete Advocacy Initiative is an activist organization that provides legal information, advice, support, and advocacy for athletes. The organization was founded in 2019 and is a product of *CBS Sports*. The organization will provide assistance for college athletes on issues involving financial aid, health and safety, and concerns about abuse or exploitation. The organization will further develop campaigns supporting athlete activism and protests and will provide pro bono legal assistance for athletes.

College Athletes Players Association (CAPA)

www.collegeathletespa.org

The CAPA is a national, nonprofit advocacy group dedicated to providing assistance and aid for college athletes at all levels. The CAPA lobbies on behalf of college sports reforms, supports and funds studies on college sports issues, and provides advocacy services for college athletes and their families. It is one of the largest mainstream organizations lobbying for compensation for college athletes.

National Association of Intercollegiate Athletics (NAIA)

www.naia.org

The NAIA is an alternative to the NCAA that serves small North American colleges and Universities. In addition to being active in the United States, the NAIA also represents colleges and universities in Canada and in the US Virgin Islands. The NAIA oversees and holds championships for men's and women's basketball, football, lacrosse, soccer, swimming, wrestling, volleyball, tennis, and track.

The National College Players Association (NCPA)

www.ncpa.org

The NCPA is a nonprofit advocacy group that provides outreach and resources for players and advocates for fair treatment of athletes. The NCPA has been involved in efforts to lobby for new rules meant to prevent or reduce the likelihood of brain injury and has also been active in campaigns to increase scholarships and stipends for student athletes.

National Collegiate Athletics Association (NCAA)

www.ncaa.com

The NCAA, started in 1906, is the nation's largest and most powerful amateur athletics organization. The NCAA represents athletes in more than 1,200 schools across the country, representing more than 200,000 student athletes. Started in 1906, the NCAA is also the most controversial of the collegiate athletics associations, largely due to the organization's management of revenues from high-profile college sports competitions. The organization frequently publishes articles and news and supports a large number of subordinate groups and organizations involved in various aspects of college athletics.

National Junior College Athletic Association (NJCAA)

www.njcaa.org

The NJCAA is a governing body that oversees sports and sports teams in junior colleges across the United States. Started in the late 1930s, the organization oversees athletes and divisions for basketball, baseball, softball, volleyball, track, soccer, tennis, wrestling, golf, football, swimming, diving, lacrosse, and several others. The NJCAA also supports research on collegiate sports and scholarships for athletes seeking to enroll in one of the nation's junior colleges.

Index